Khristina Reed Manansala
Art Gallery Book-1

Thank You and Welcome! Khristina Reed Manansala is a grand-daughter of the Philippine National Artist Vicente Manansala, the famous mural painter and abstract illustrator. This art book is suitable as coffee table book to entertain friends. Viewers can order the actual paintings from Khristina in Manila. She is also ready to do commission works. Each page is 8.5x11 inches, and can be cut out for framing.

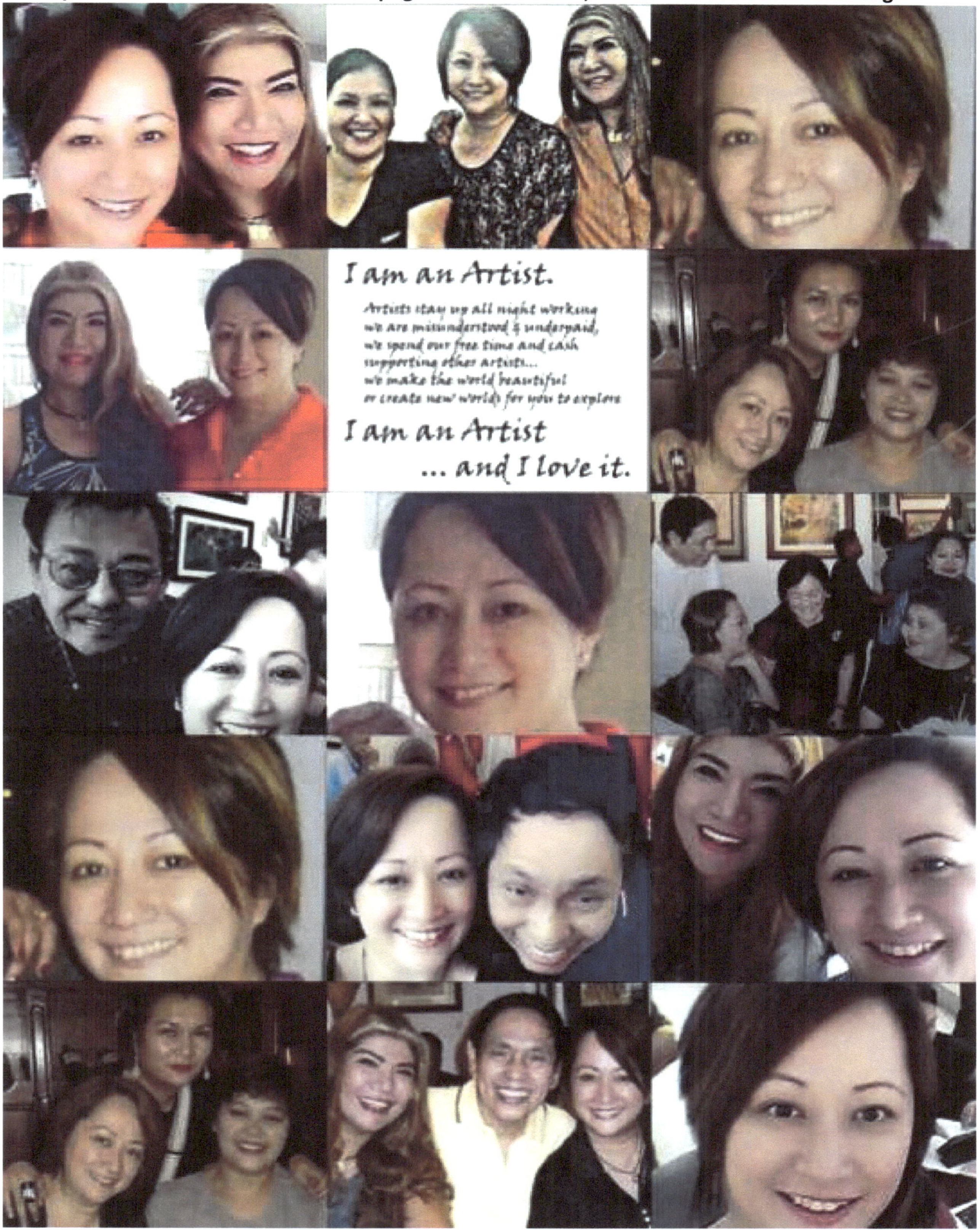

I am an Artist.

Artists stay up all night working
we are misunderstood & underpaid,
we spend our free time and cash
supporting other Artists...
we make the world beautiful
or create new worlds for you to explore

I am an Artist

... and I love it.

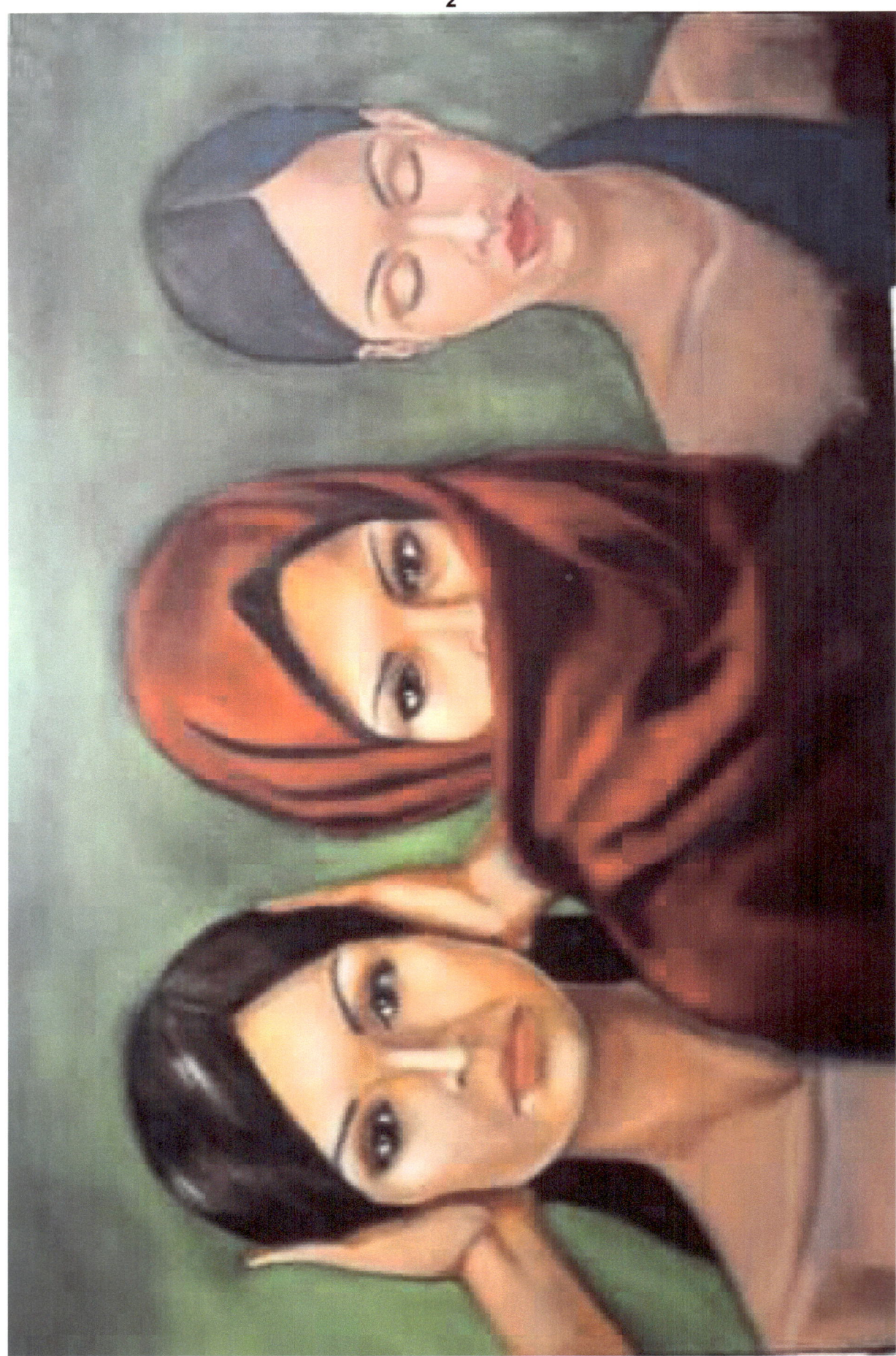

A Khristina Reed Manansala Painting

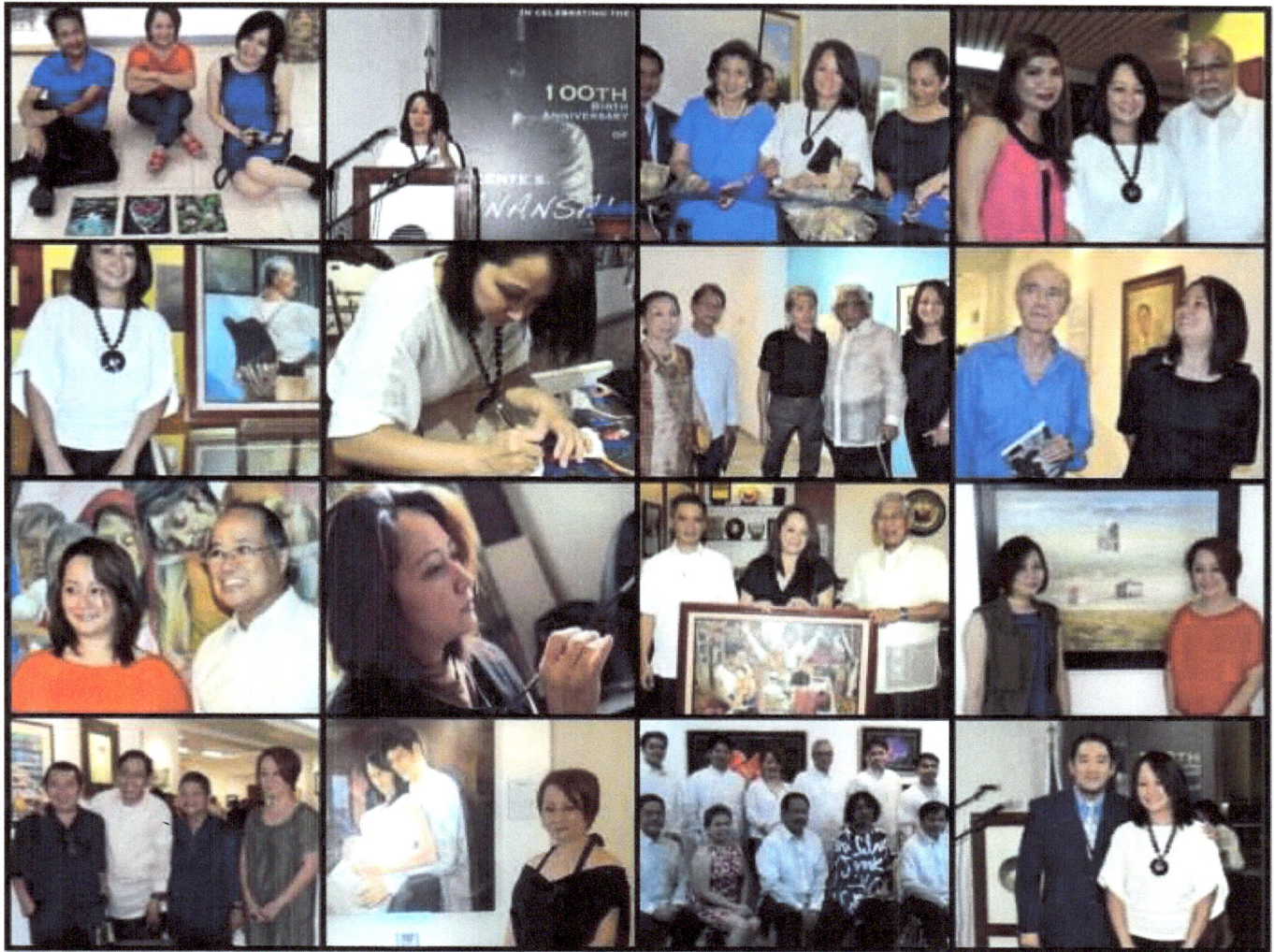

About Khristina Reed Manansala

Born in Manila; The Philippines. Coming from a world renowned innovator of visual art, Manansala demonstrated a natural artistic ability since she was a child but never encouraged to pursue art professionally. For someone with such noticeable early talent it is surprising, that it's only in the last four years she seriously considered art as a means of living and moved to painting full-time. It is perhaps understandable for someone of her generation to consider the pressures of todays' life before stepping out of the comfort zone of living the corporate lifestyle. We must admit that only a remarkable few have made it in the books of history. The sad truth is; most are soon forgotten and never leave their mark.

Since her return to her original passion, Manansala came a long way in the notoriously hard to crack art world. Initially, she established a studio in Mandaluyong City and became a regular member of the Art Association of the Philippines and Tuesday Group of Artists respectively. The said group would have weekly On-The-Spot painting sessions and monthly exhibitions; she now creates art in her studio in Las Pinas City, a place she grew up as a child fired with her passion to recreate images perceived by her mind.

Most of her work focuses on religious subjects; reminiscent of her childhood as she runs through the hallways that are filled with the magnificent works of her forefather, like the Crucifixion and Madonna and Child. Manansala's work can be found in private art collections both in the Philippines and abroad, and has participated in numerous exhibitions nationwide. Recent group exhibitions include Canvas Group Exhibit in Manila Hotel, Tuesday Group Annual Exhibit. Fort Santiago, Art 19b Exhibit, Akwarelista sa Emerald, and Phil-Korean International Exhibit at GSIS Museum. Her works have been published in the coveted book The Great Themes in Philippine's Art: Mother and Child by the late Manuel Duldulao and GSIS Art Collections.

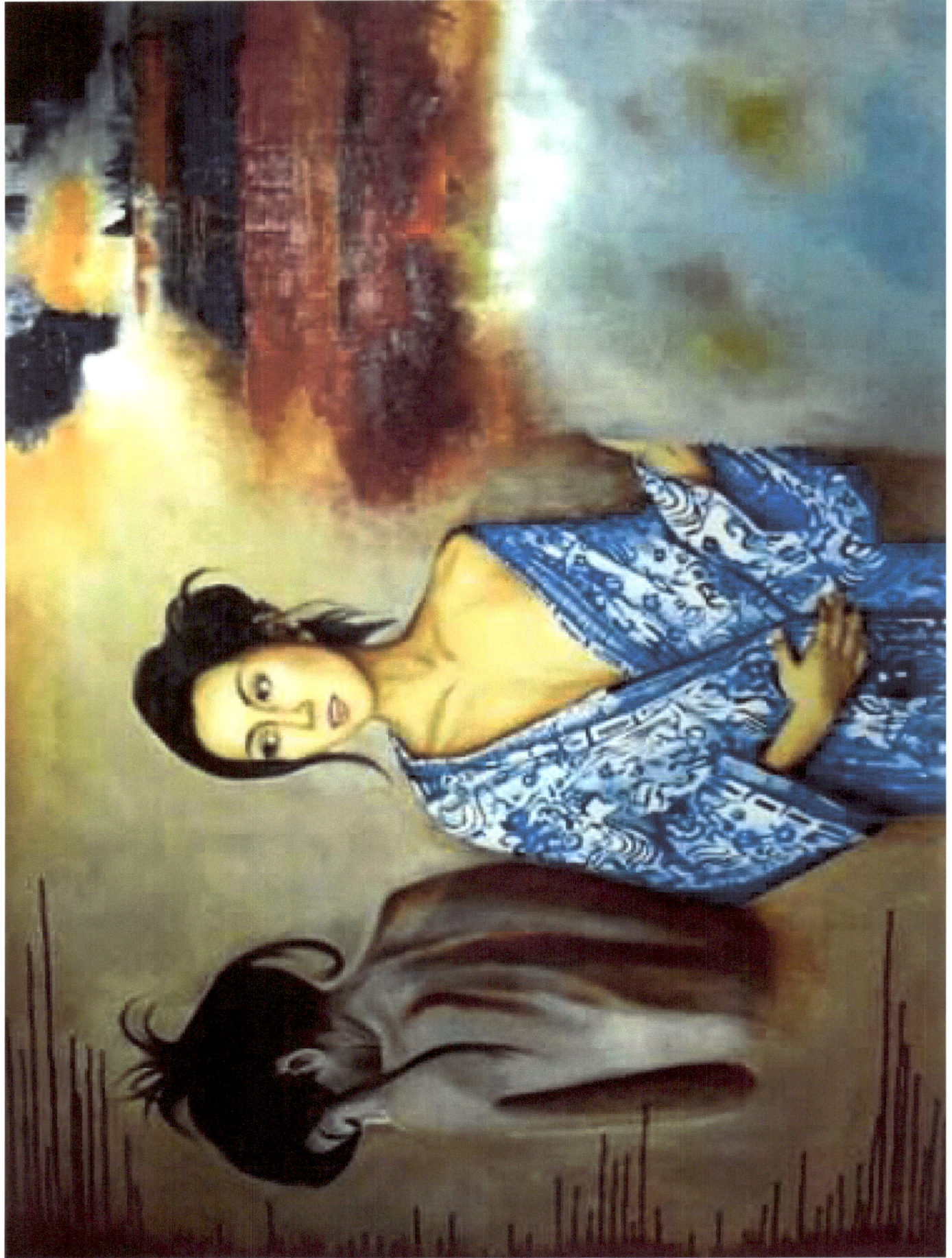

A Khristina Reed Manansala Painting

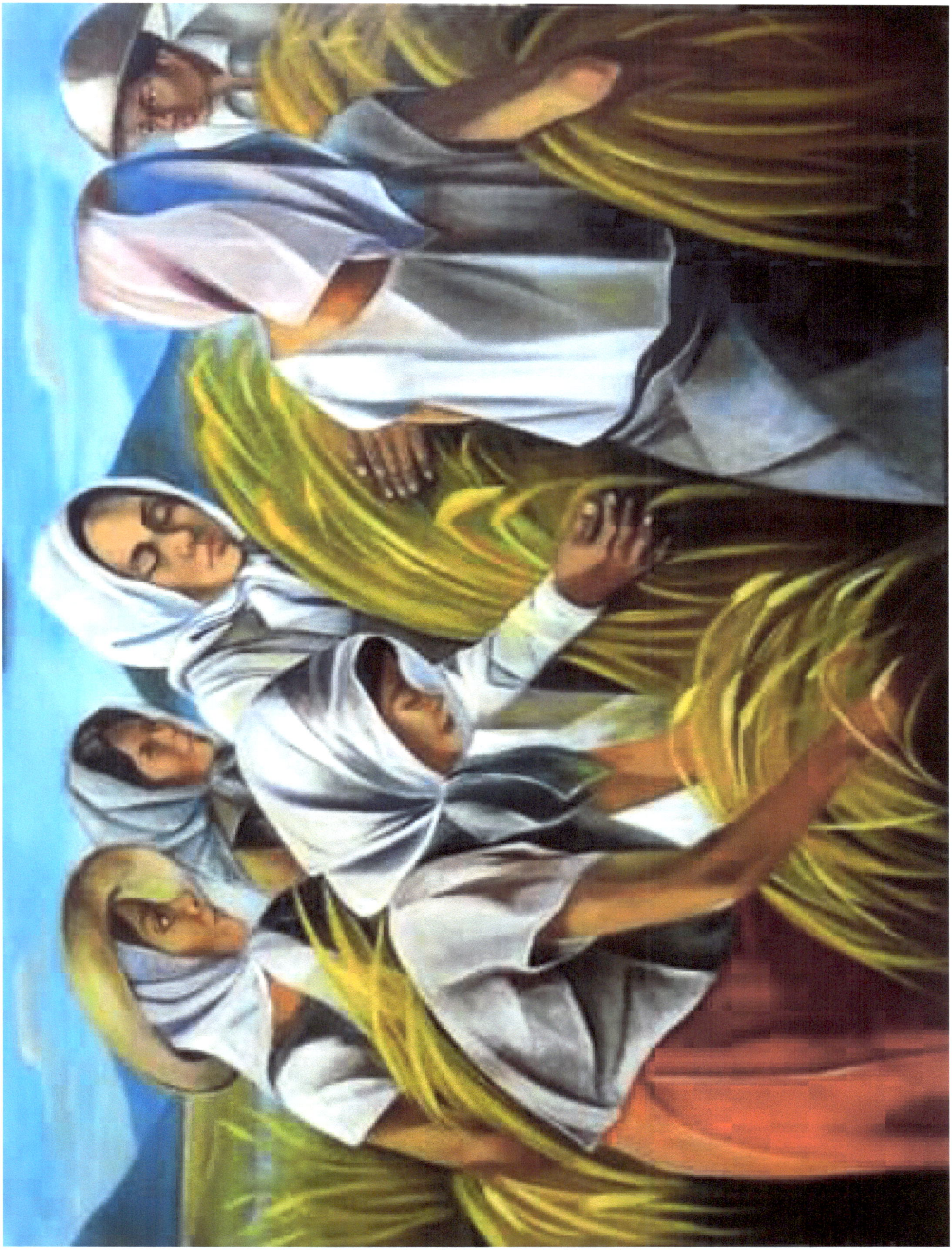

A Khristina Reed Manansala Painting

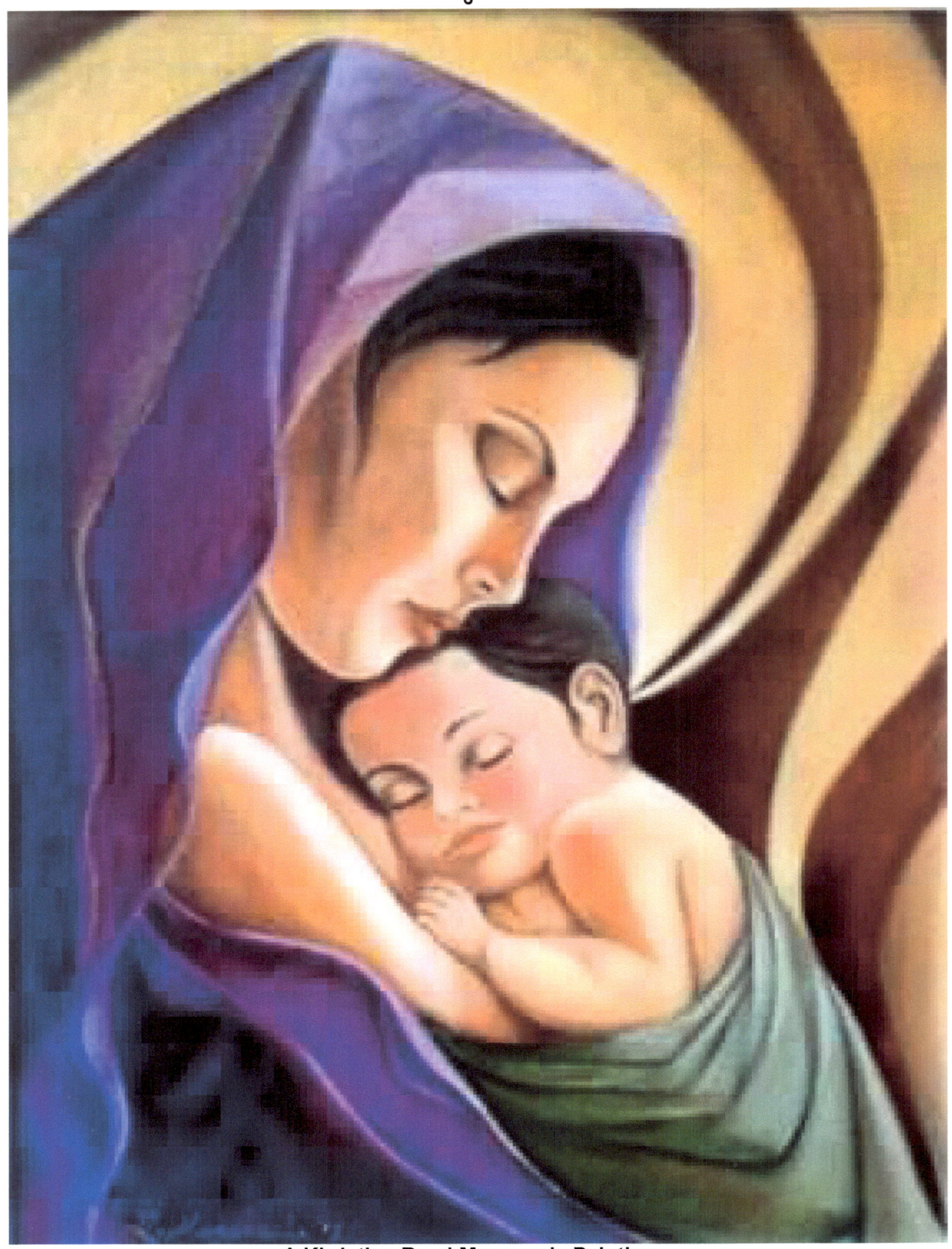

A Khristina Reed Manansala Painting

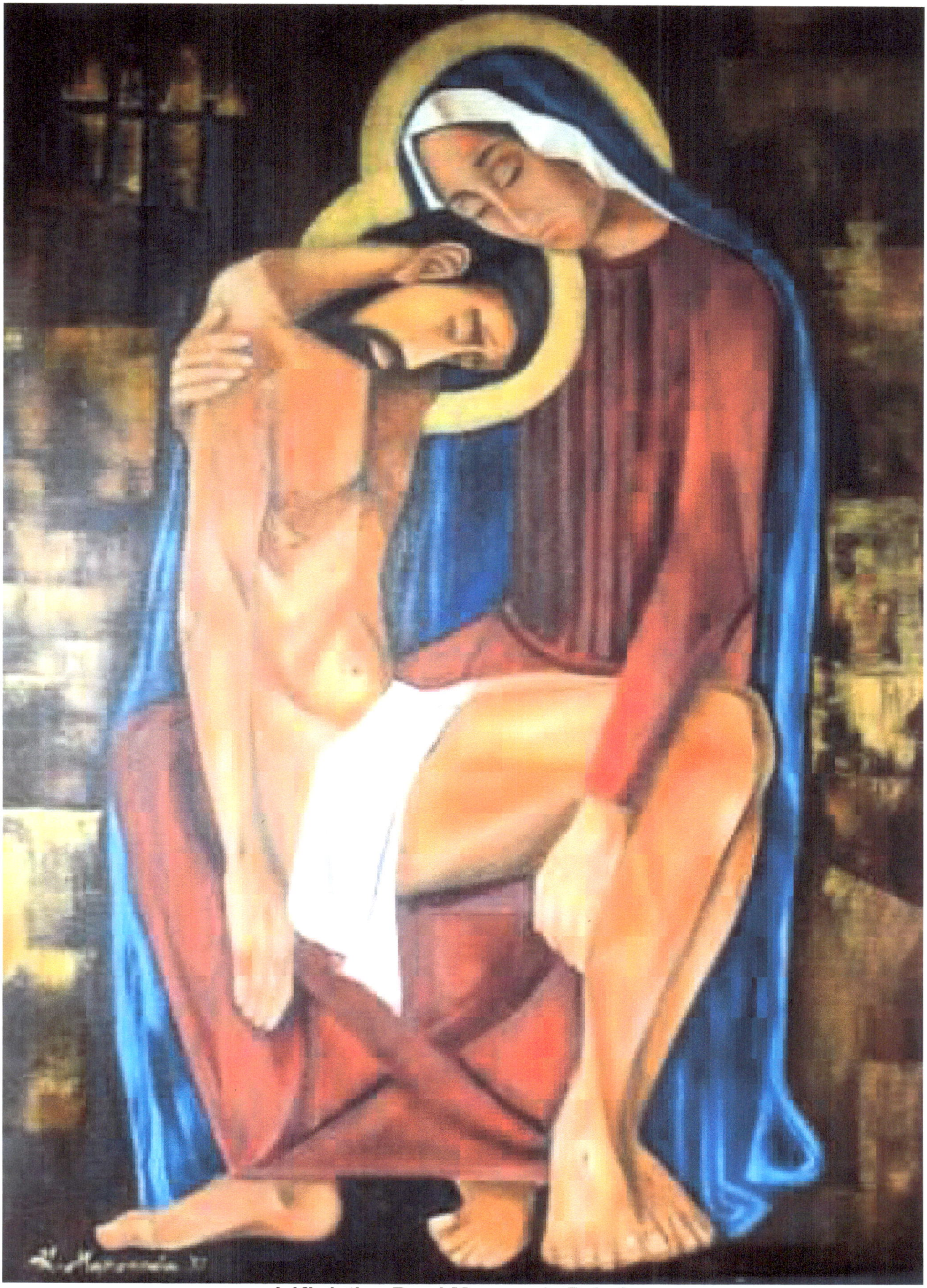

A Khristina Reed Manansala Painting

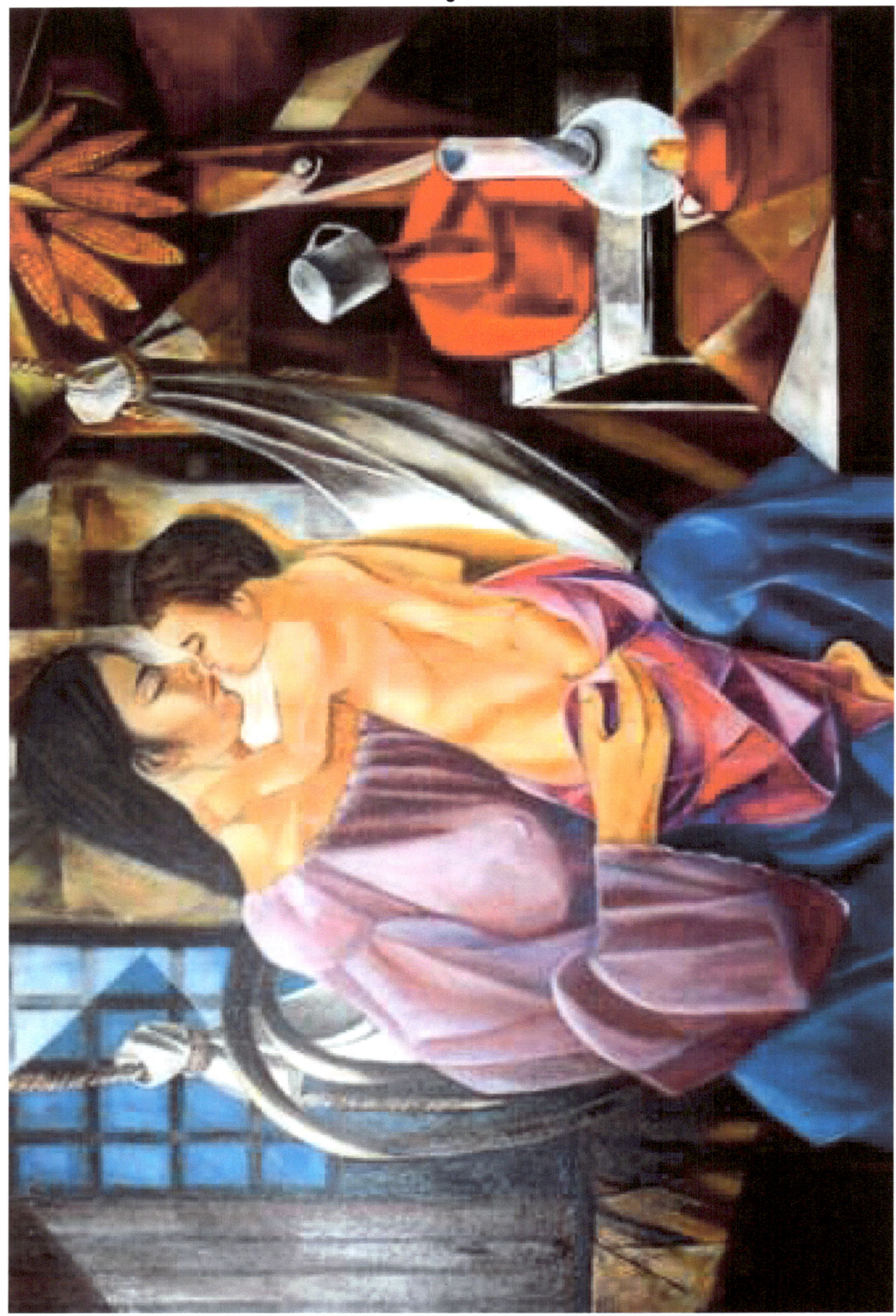

A Khristina Reed Manansala Painting

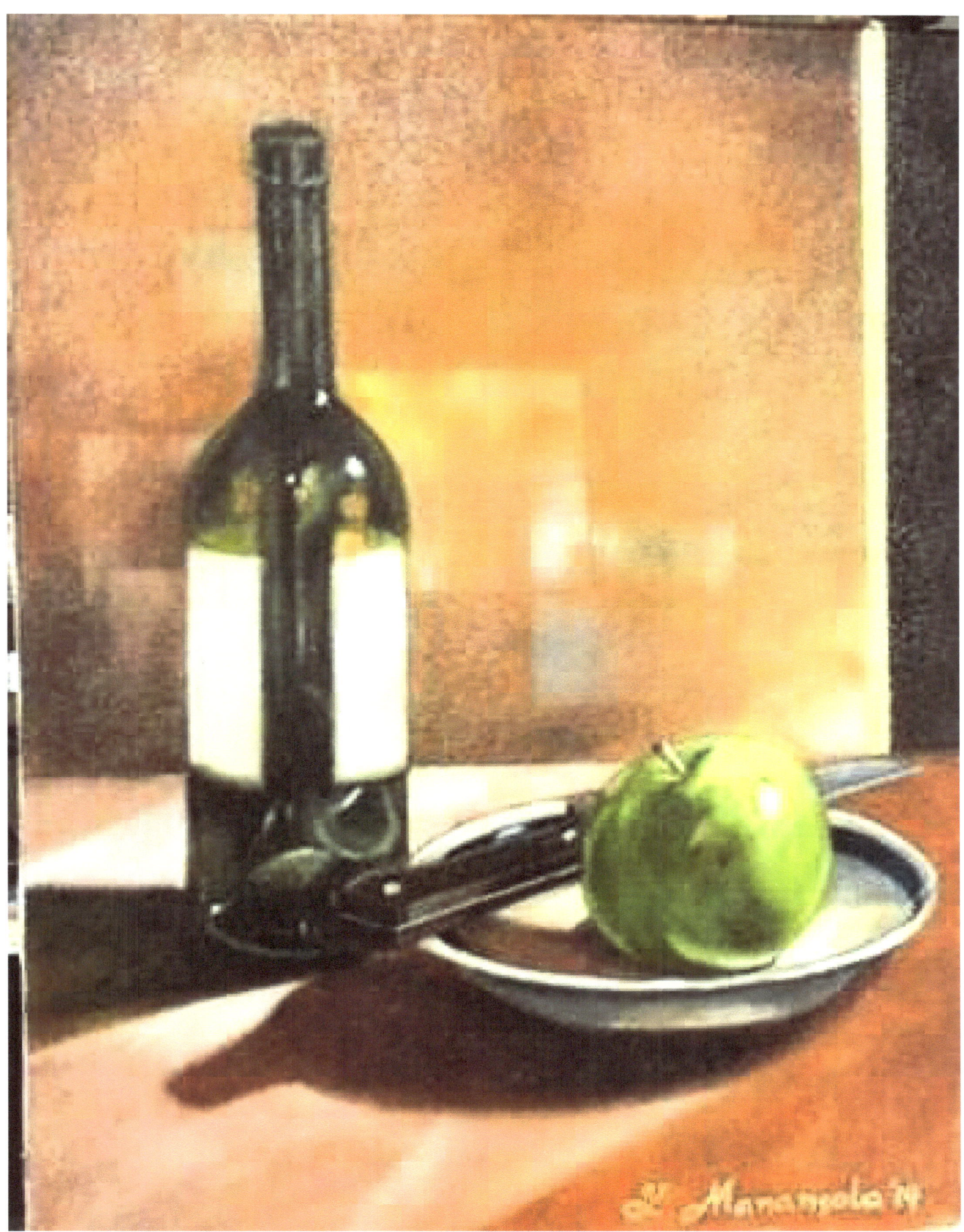

A Khristina Reed Manansala Painting

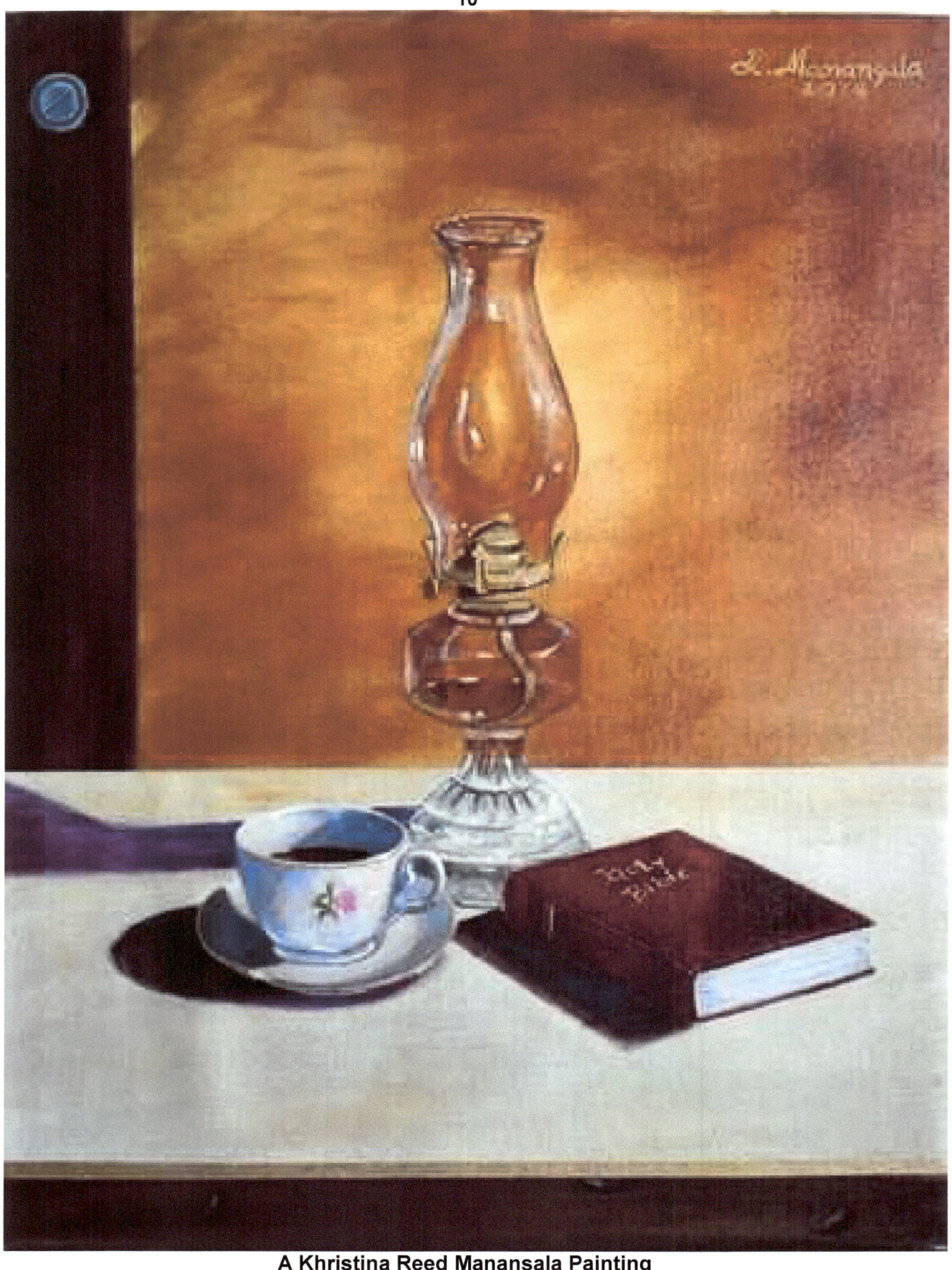

A Khristina Reed Manansala Painting

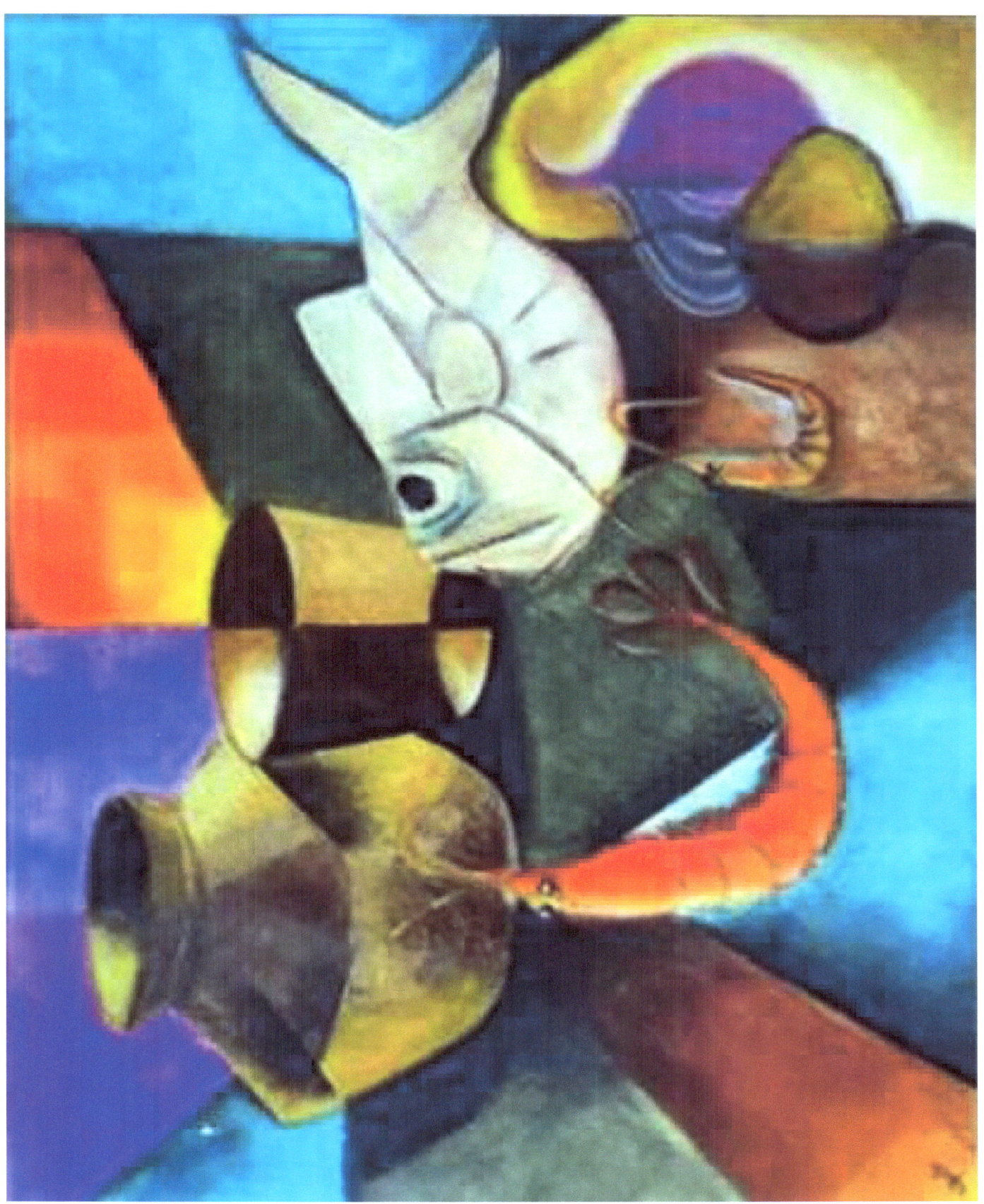

A Khristina Reed Manansala Painting

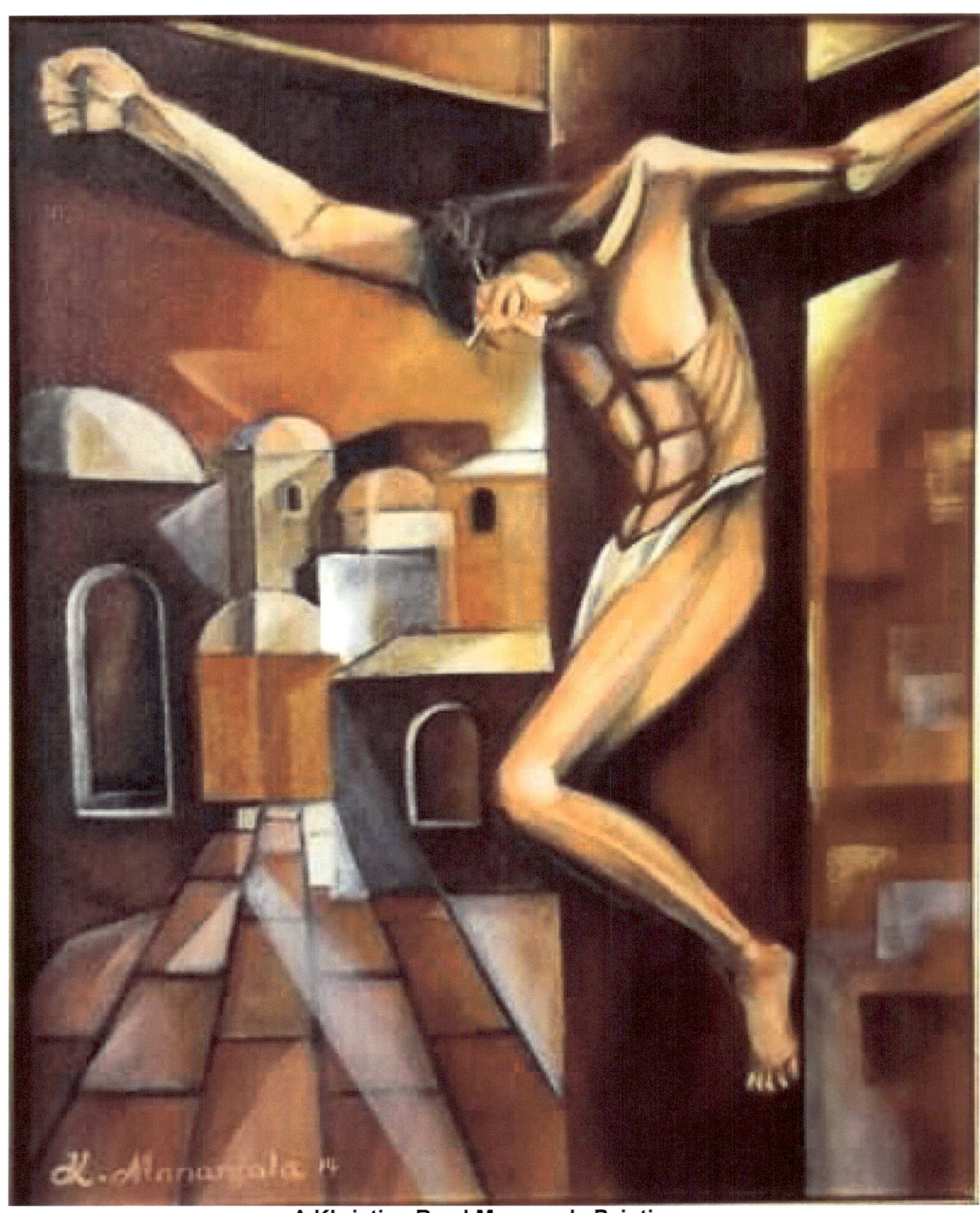

A Khristina Reed Manansala Painting

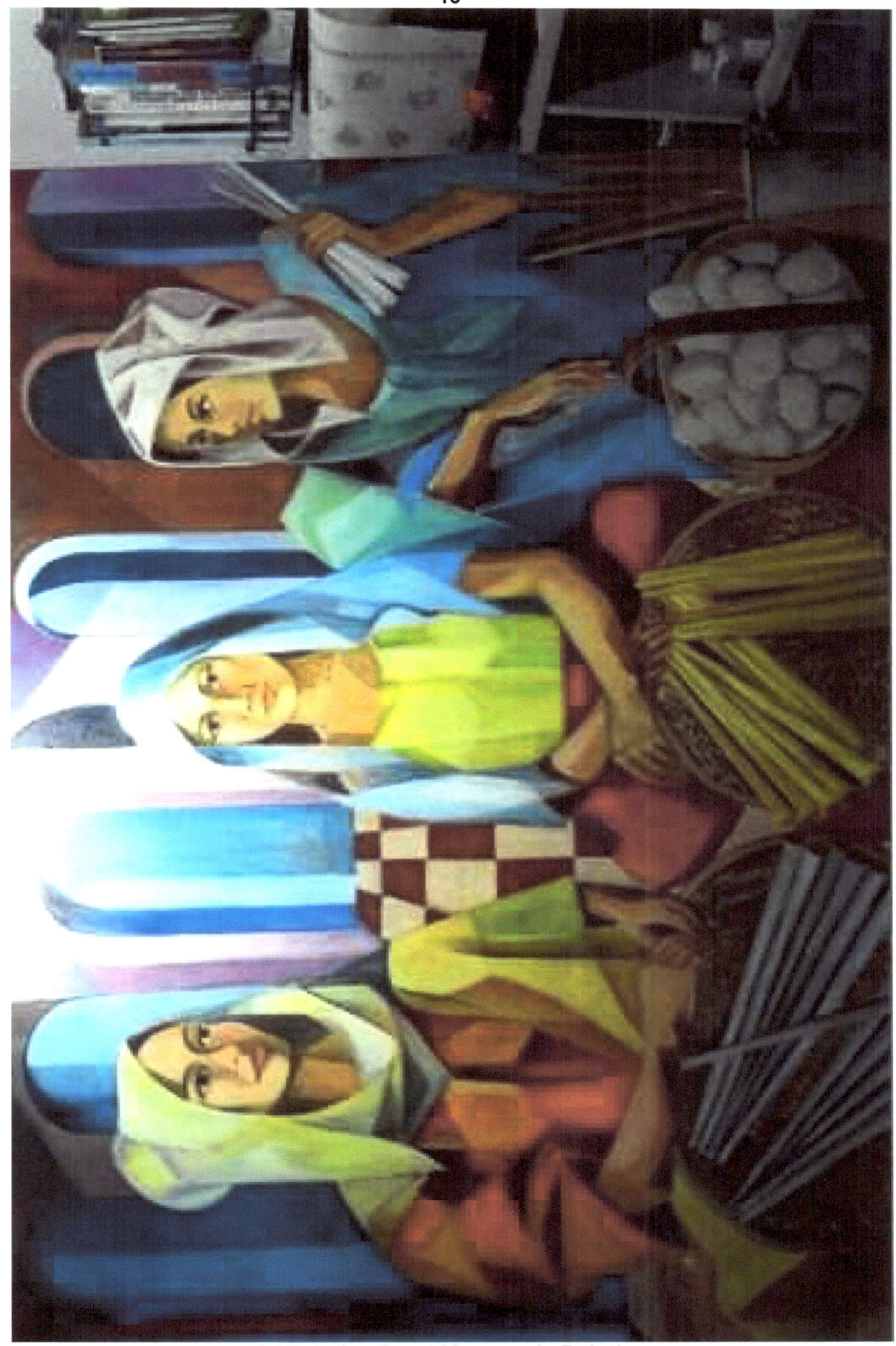

A Khristina Reed Manansala Painting

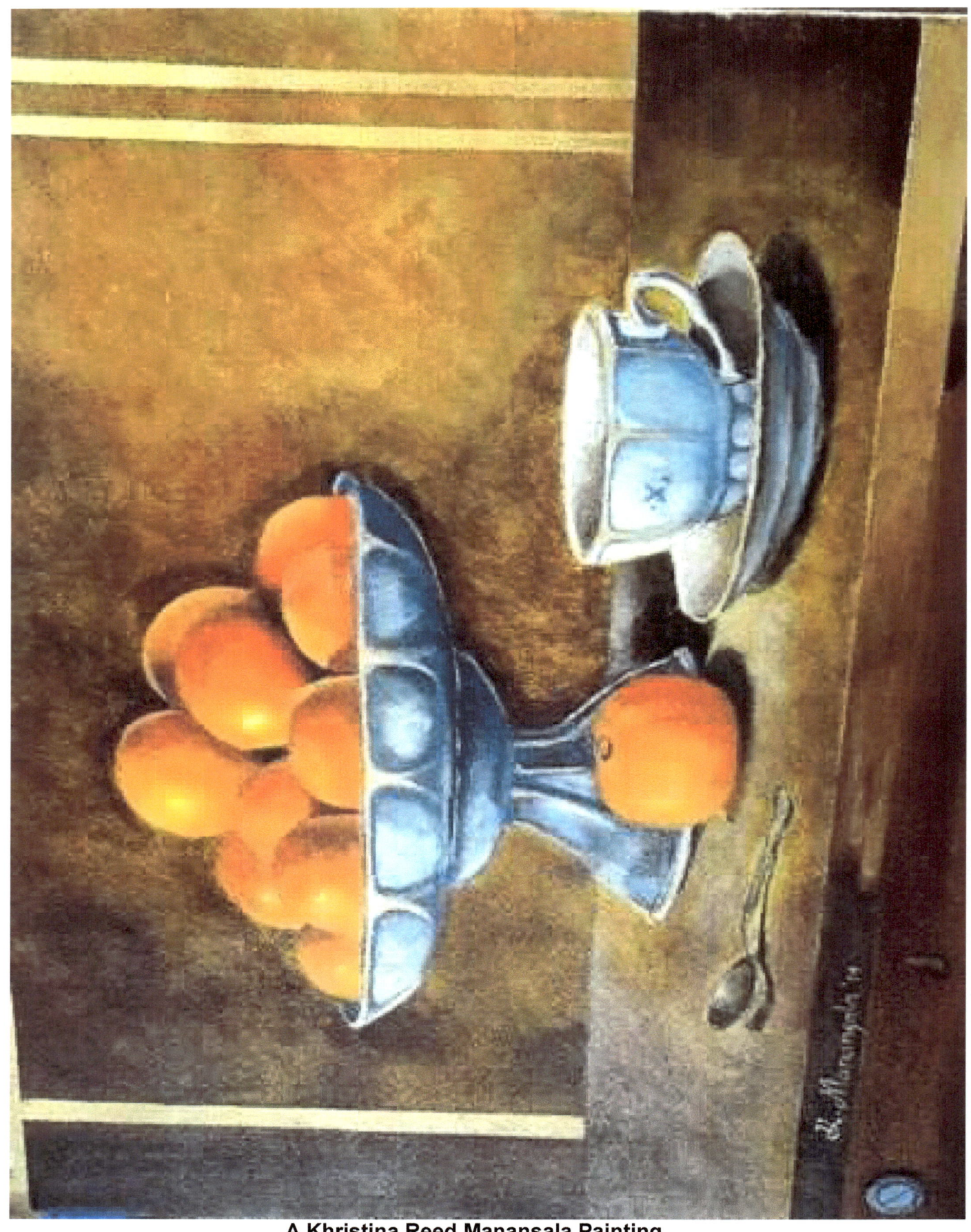

A Khristina Reed Manansala Painting

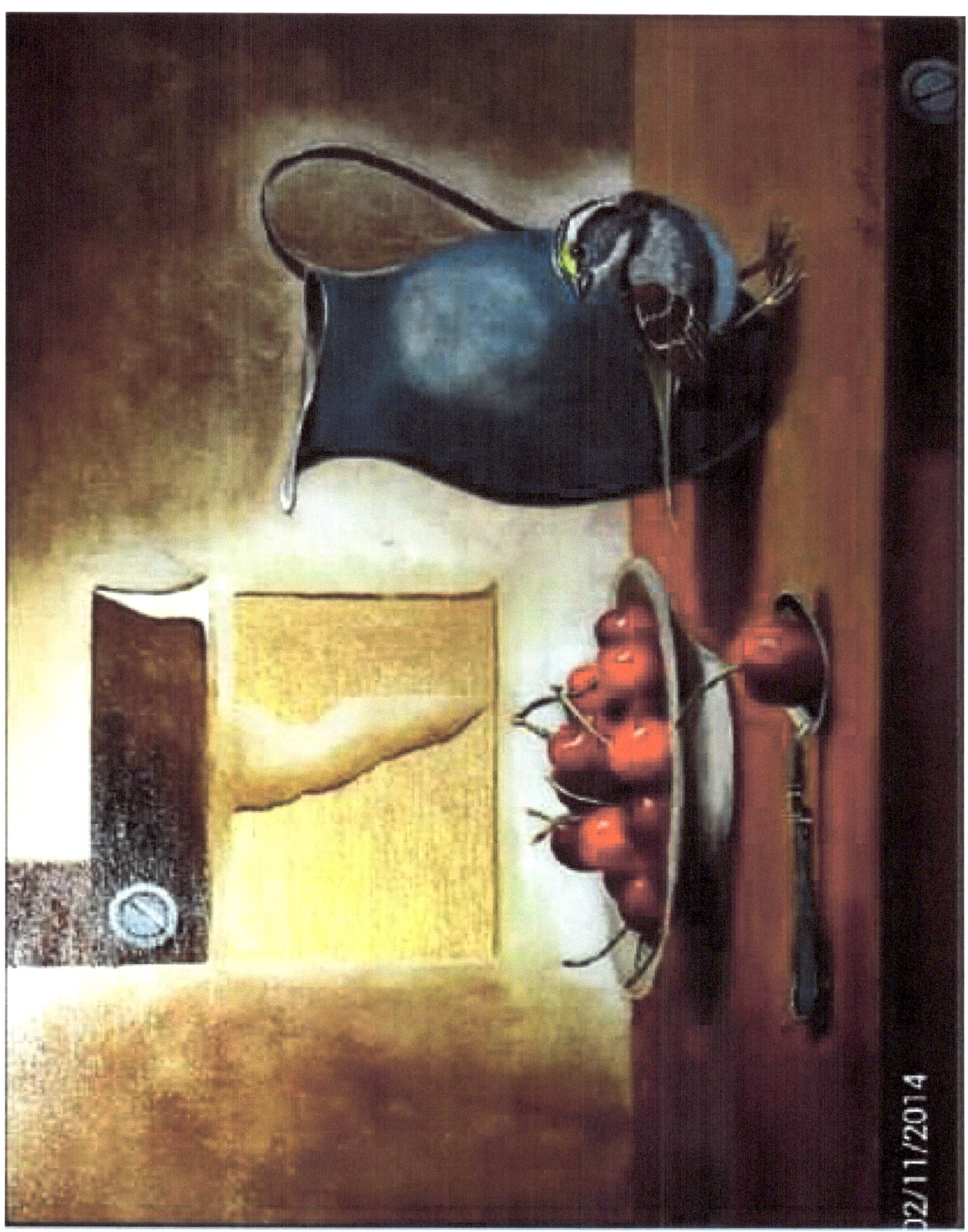

A Khristina Reed Manansala Painting

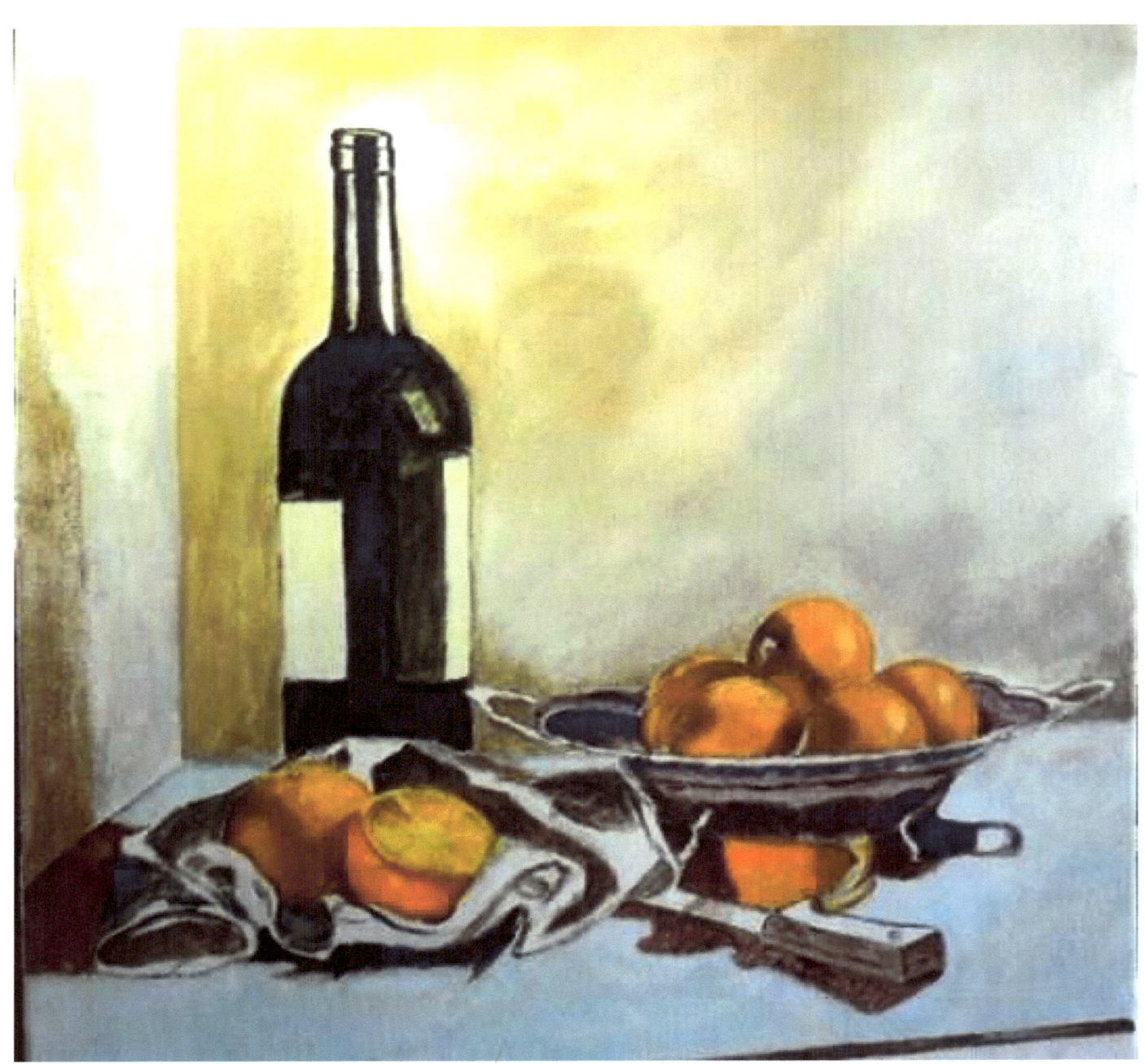

A Khristina Reed Manansala Painting

Thank You and Welcome! Khristina Reed Manansala is a grand-daughter of the Philippine National Artist Vicente Manansala, the famous mural painter and abstract illustrator. This art book is suitable as coffee table book to entertain friends. Viewers can order the actual paintings from Khristina in Manila. She is also ready to do commission works. Each page is 8.5x11 inches, and can be cut out for framing.

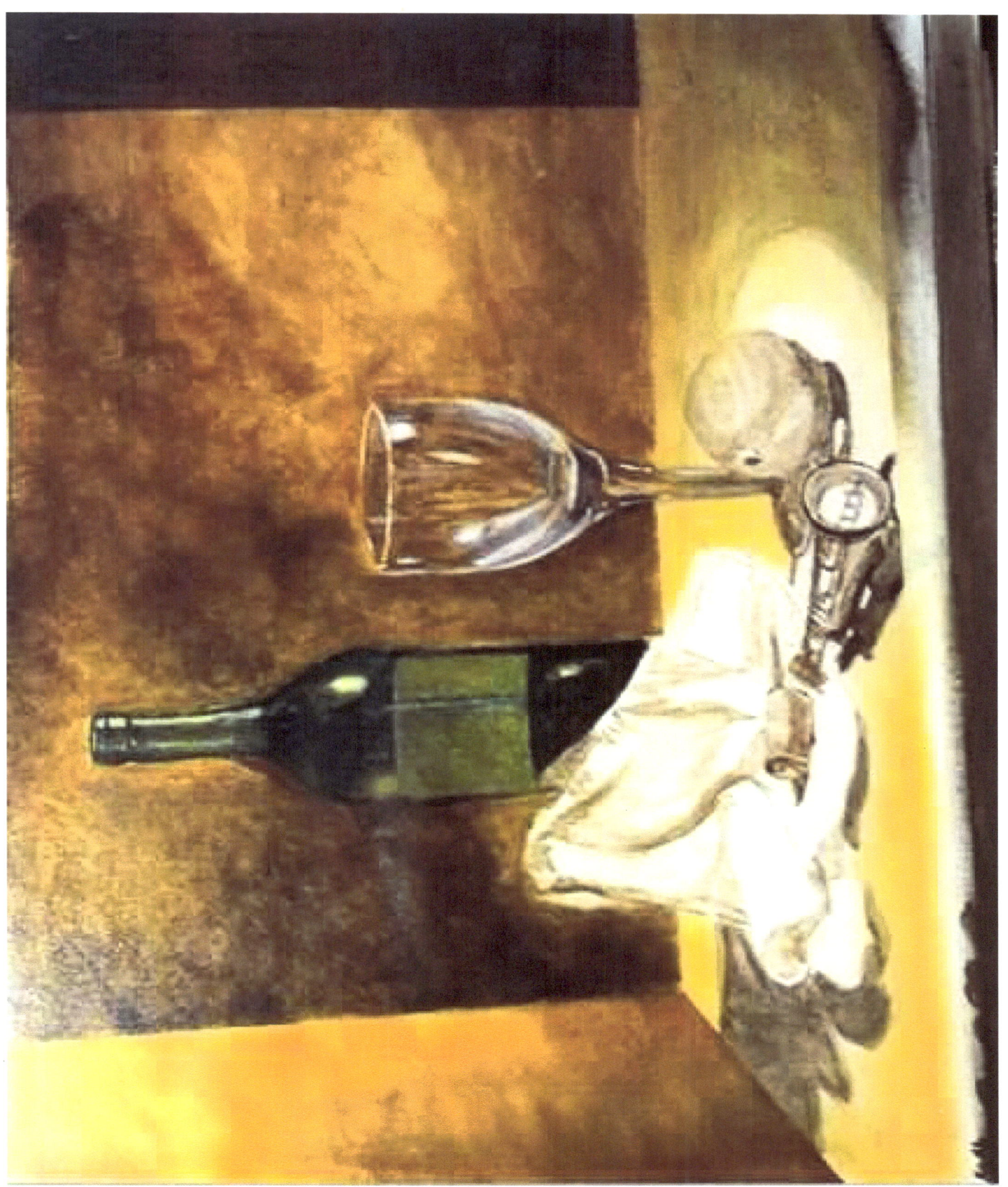

A Khristina Reed Manansala Painting

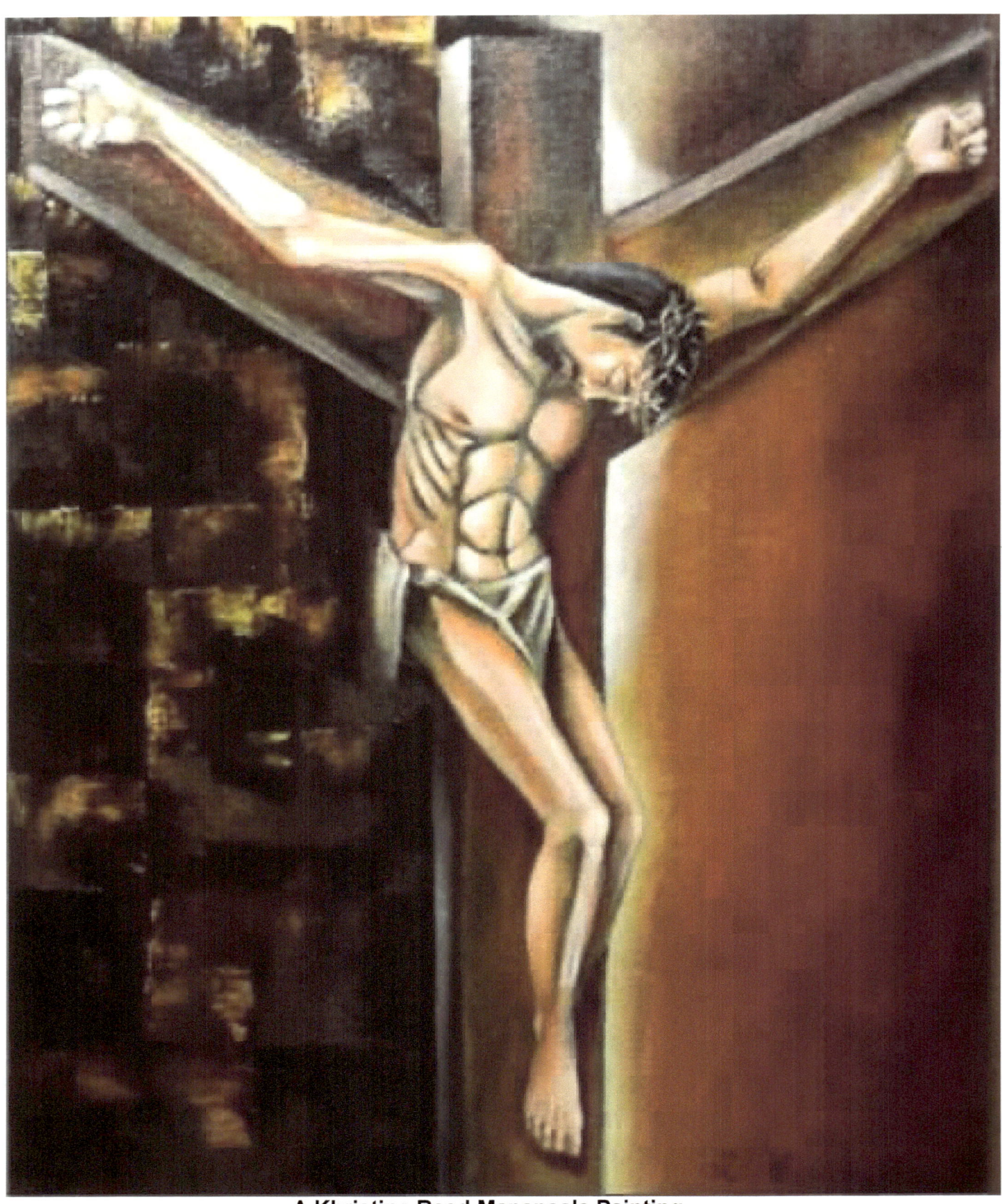

A Khristina Reed Manansala Painting

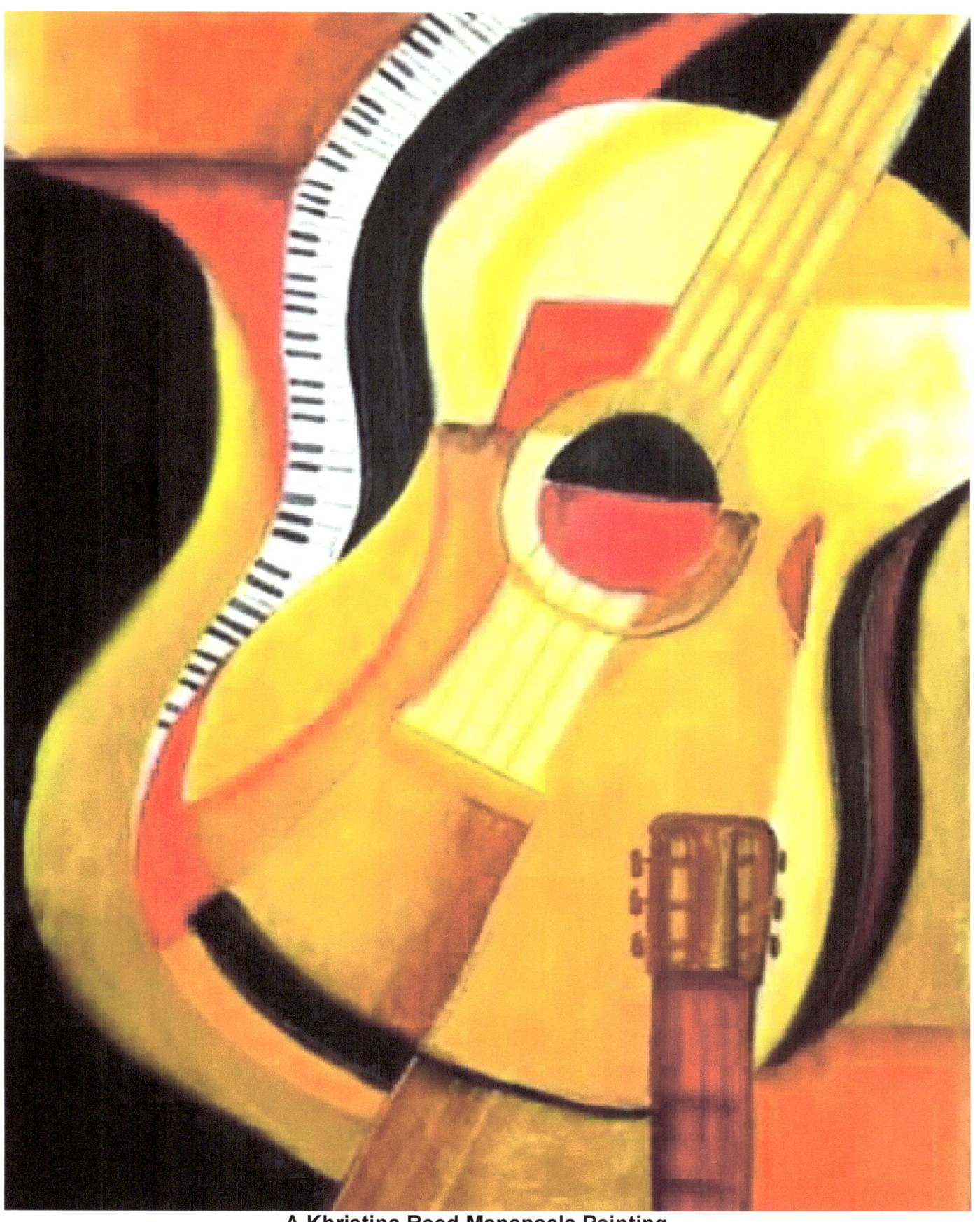

A Khristina Reed Manansala Painting

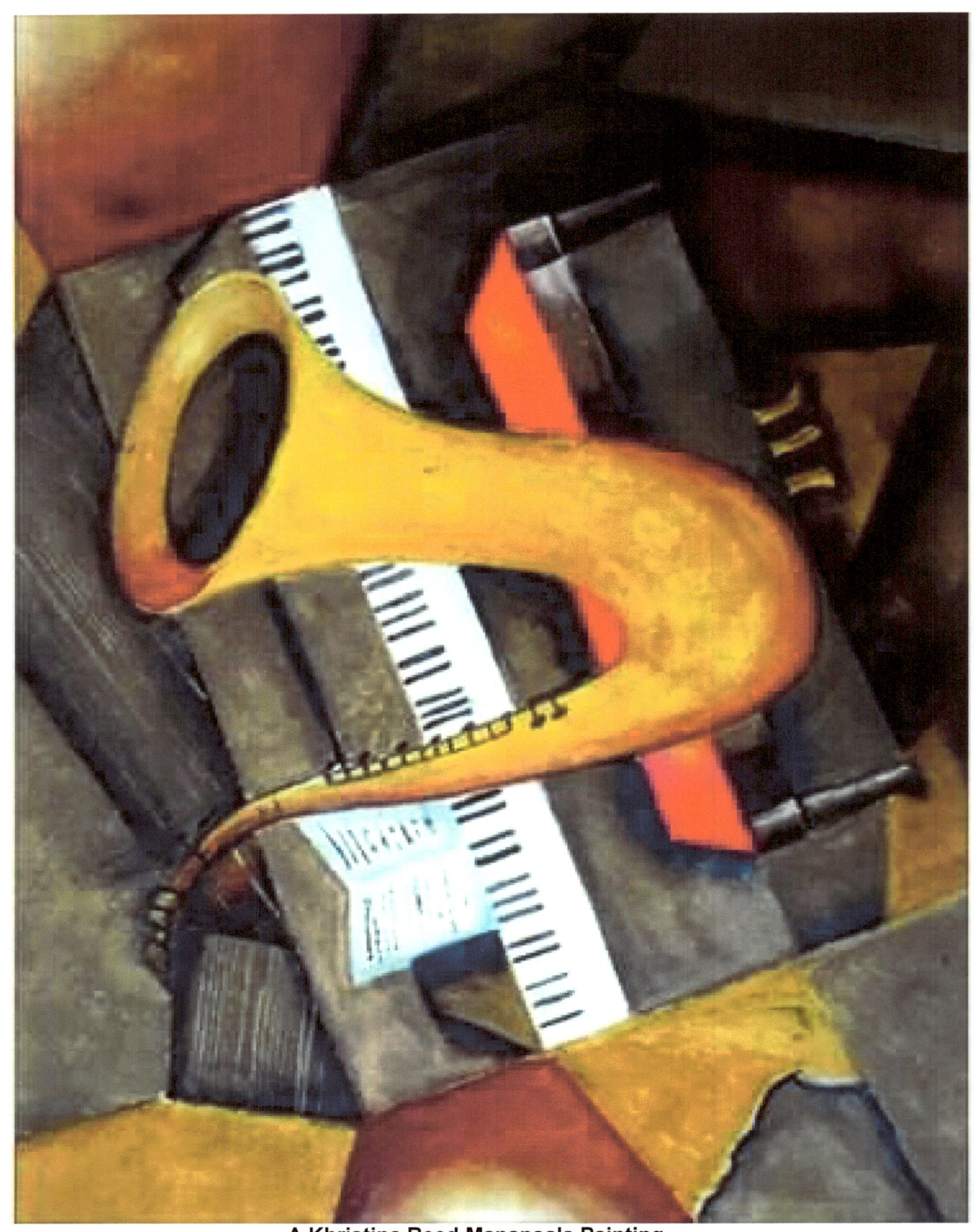

A Khristina Reed Manansala Painting

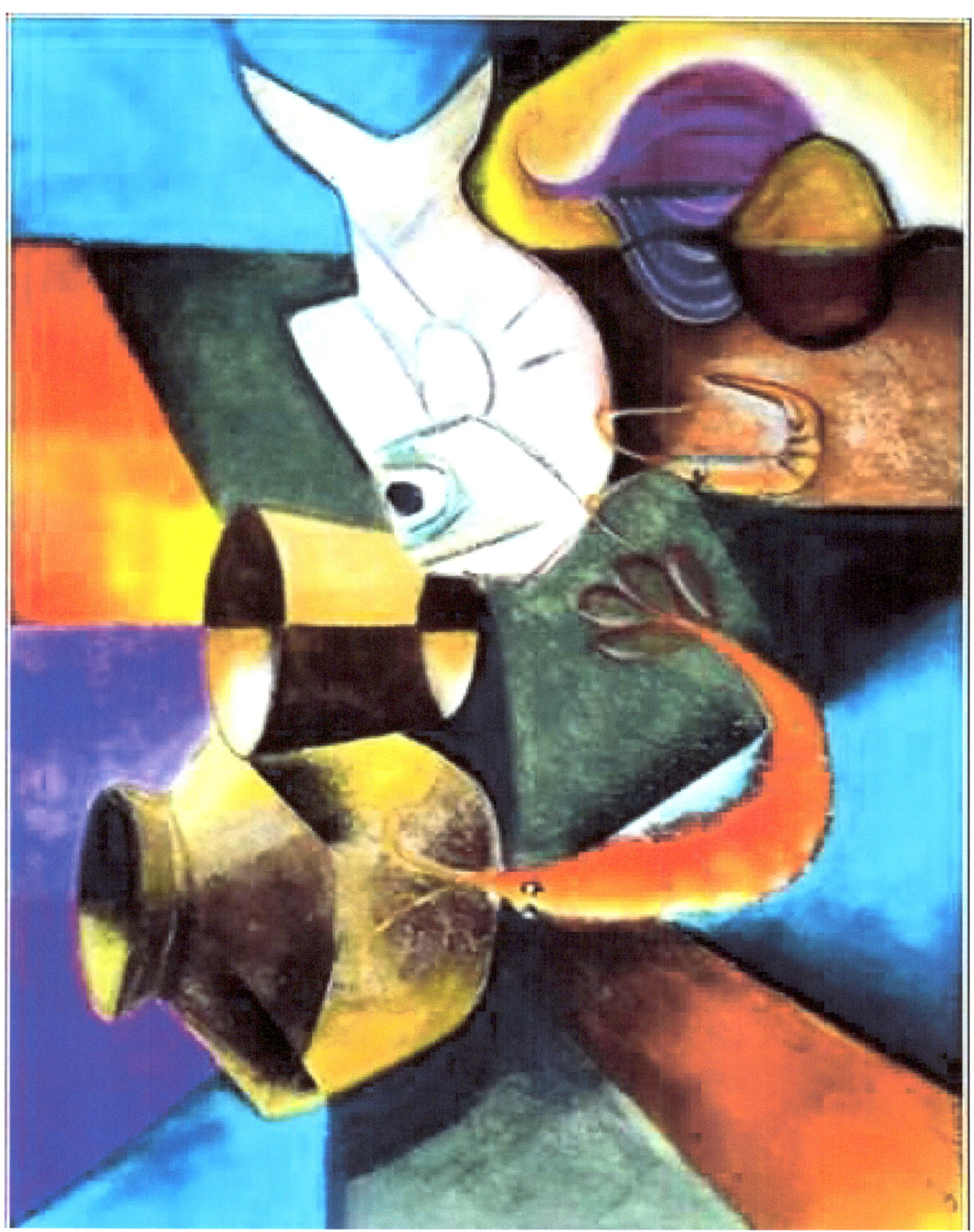

A Khristina Reed Manansala Painting

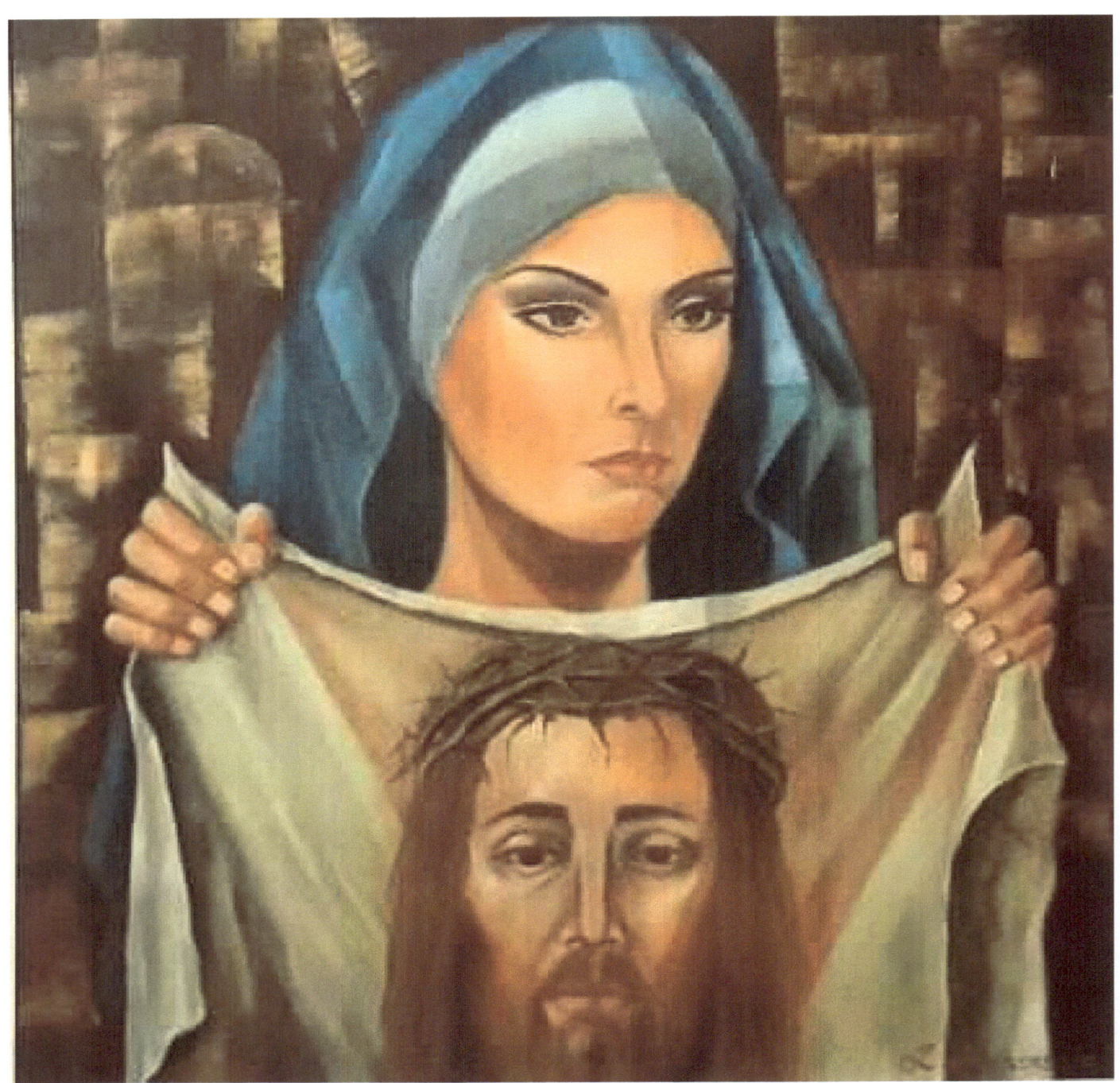

A Khristina Reed Manansala Painting

Thank You and Welcome! Khristina Reed Manansala is a grand-daughter of the Philippine National Artist Vicente Manansala, the famous mural painter and abstract illustrator. This art book is suitable as coffee table book to entertain friends. Viewers can order the actual paintings from Khristina in Manila. She is also ready to do commission works. Each page is 8.5x11 inches, and can be cut out for framing.

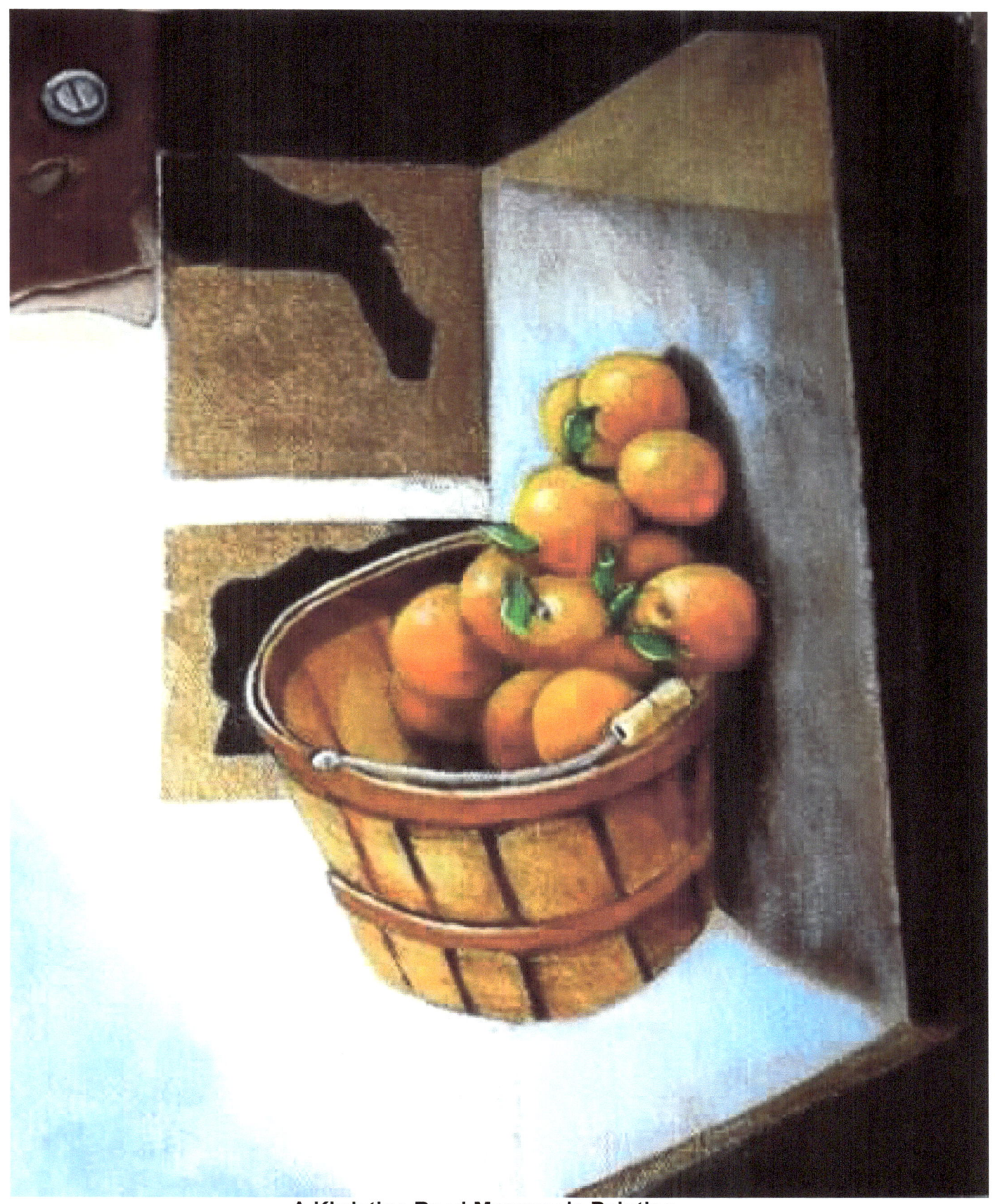

A Khristina Reed Manansala Painting

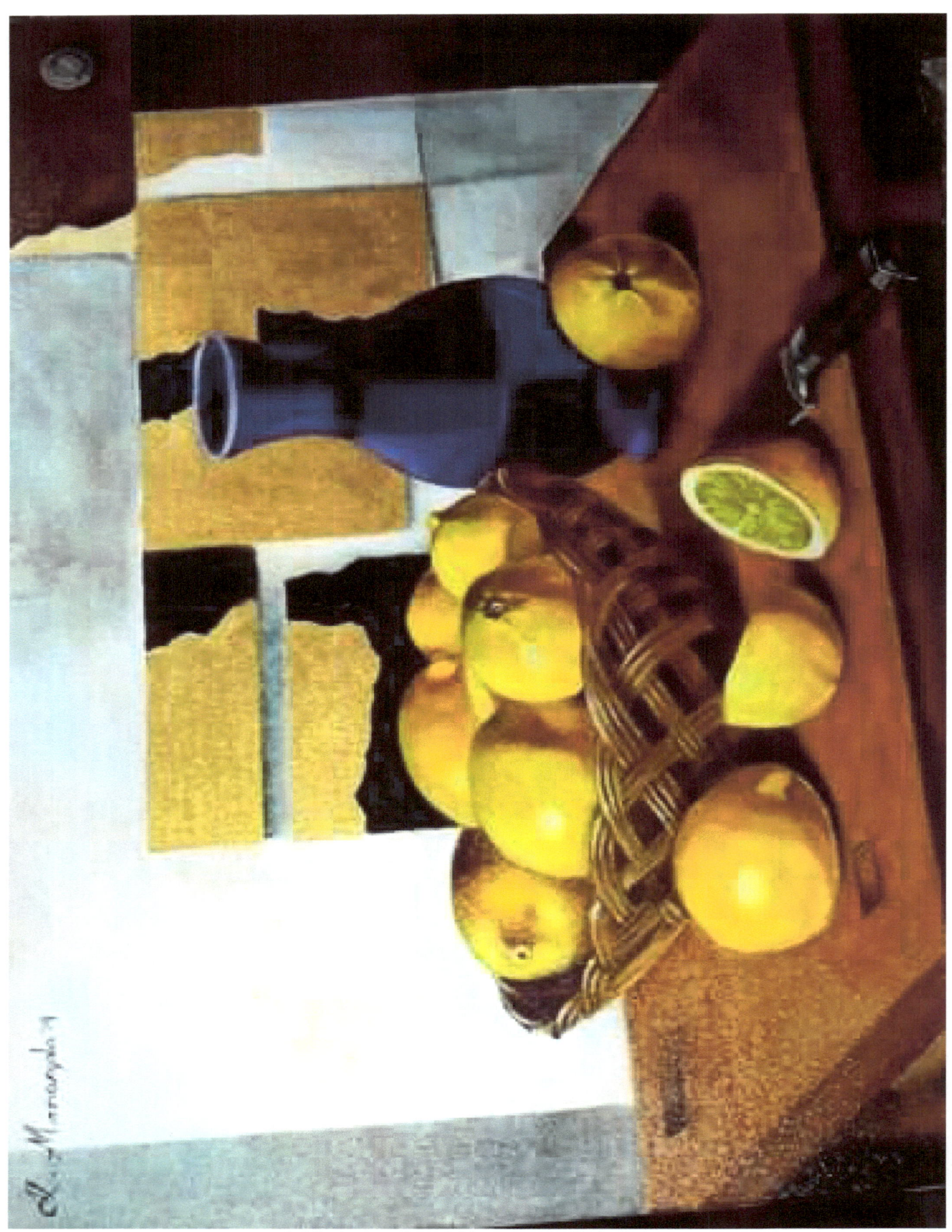

A Khristina Reed Manansala Painting

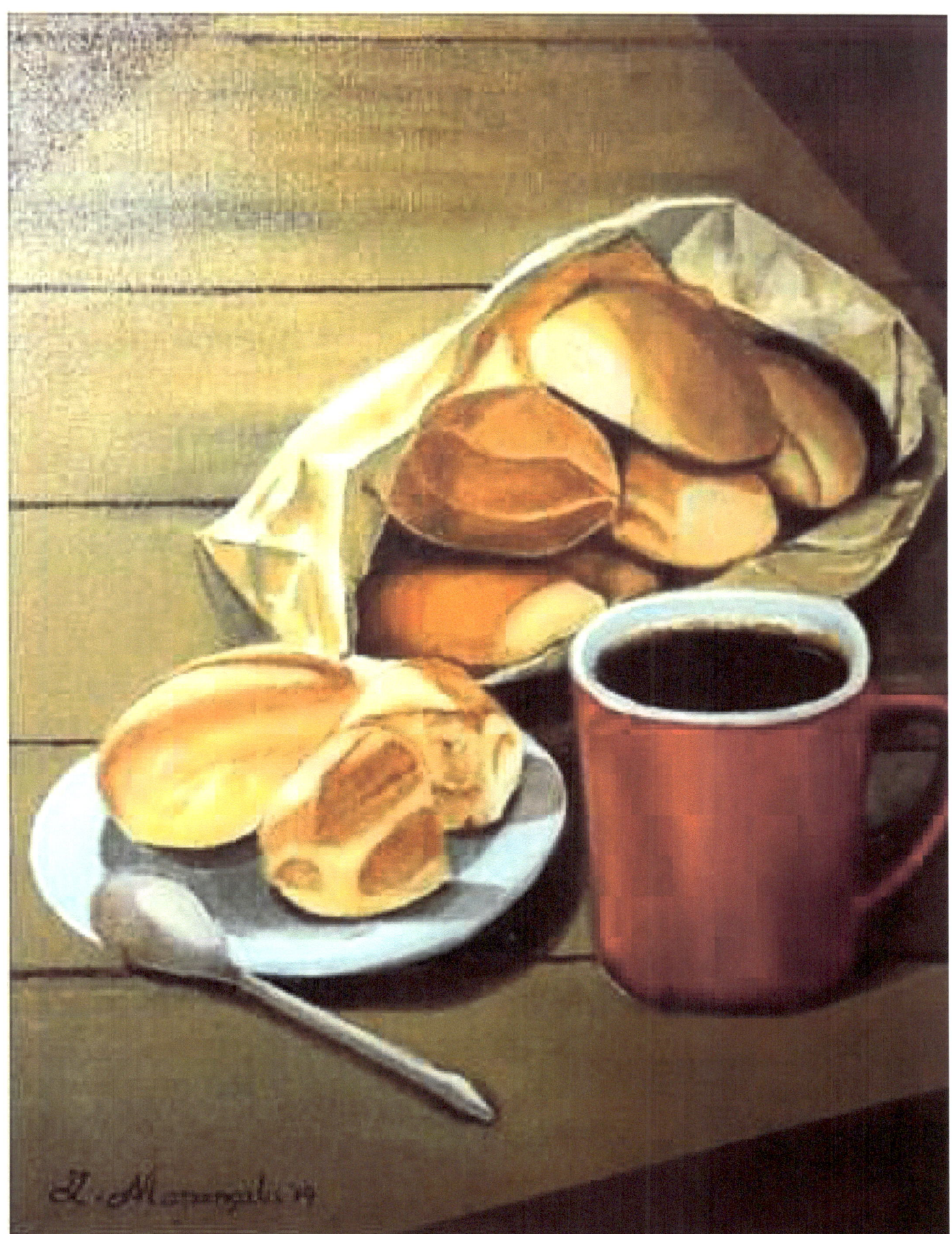

A Khristina Reed Manansala Painting

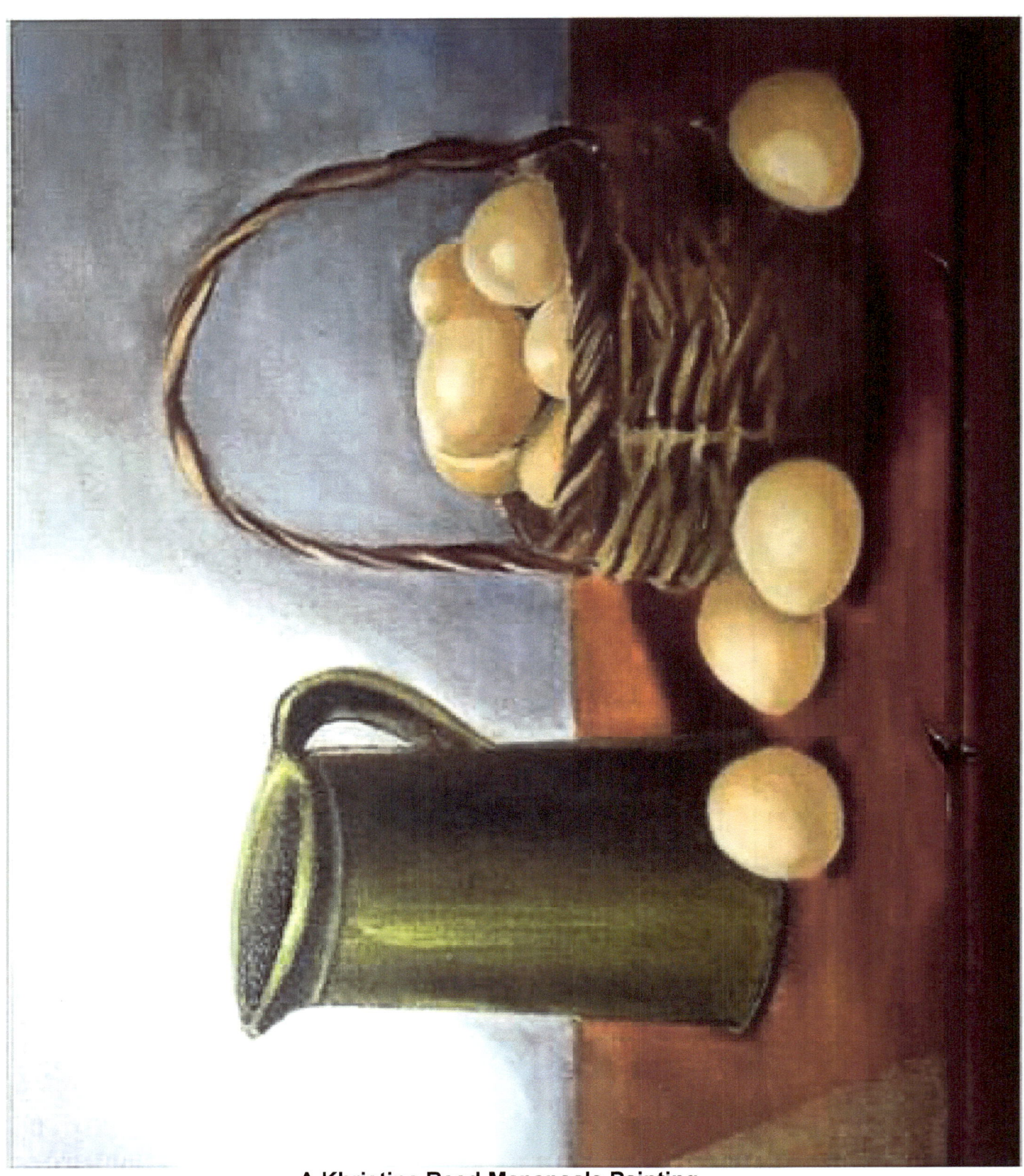

A Khristina Reed Manansala Painting

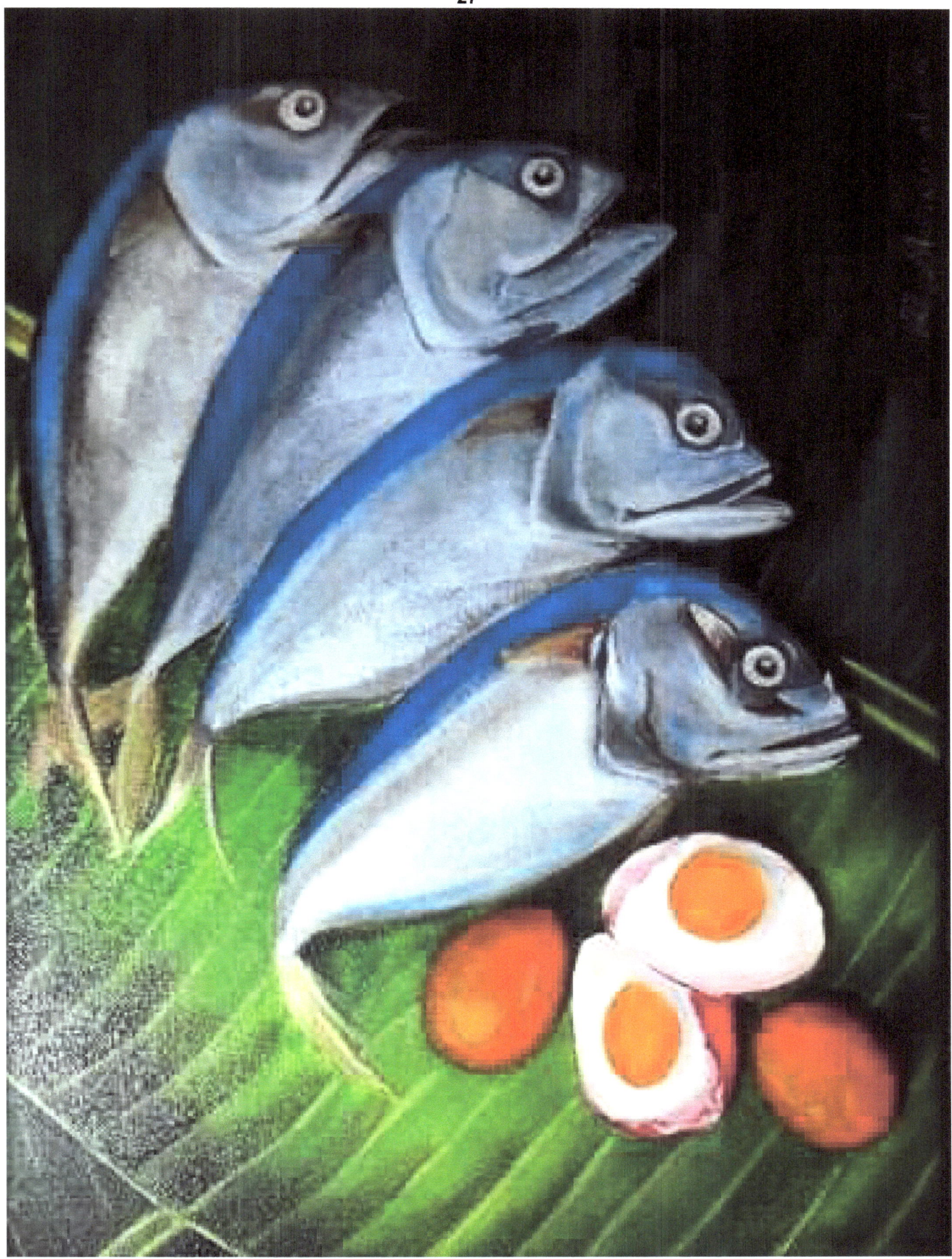

A Khristina Reed Manansala Painting

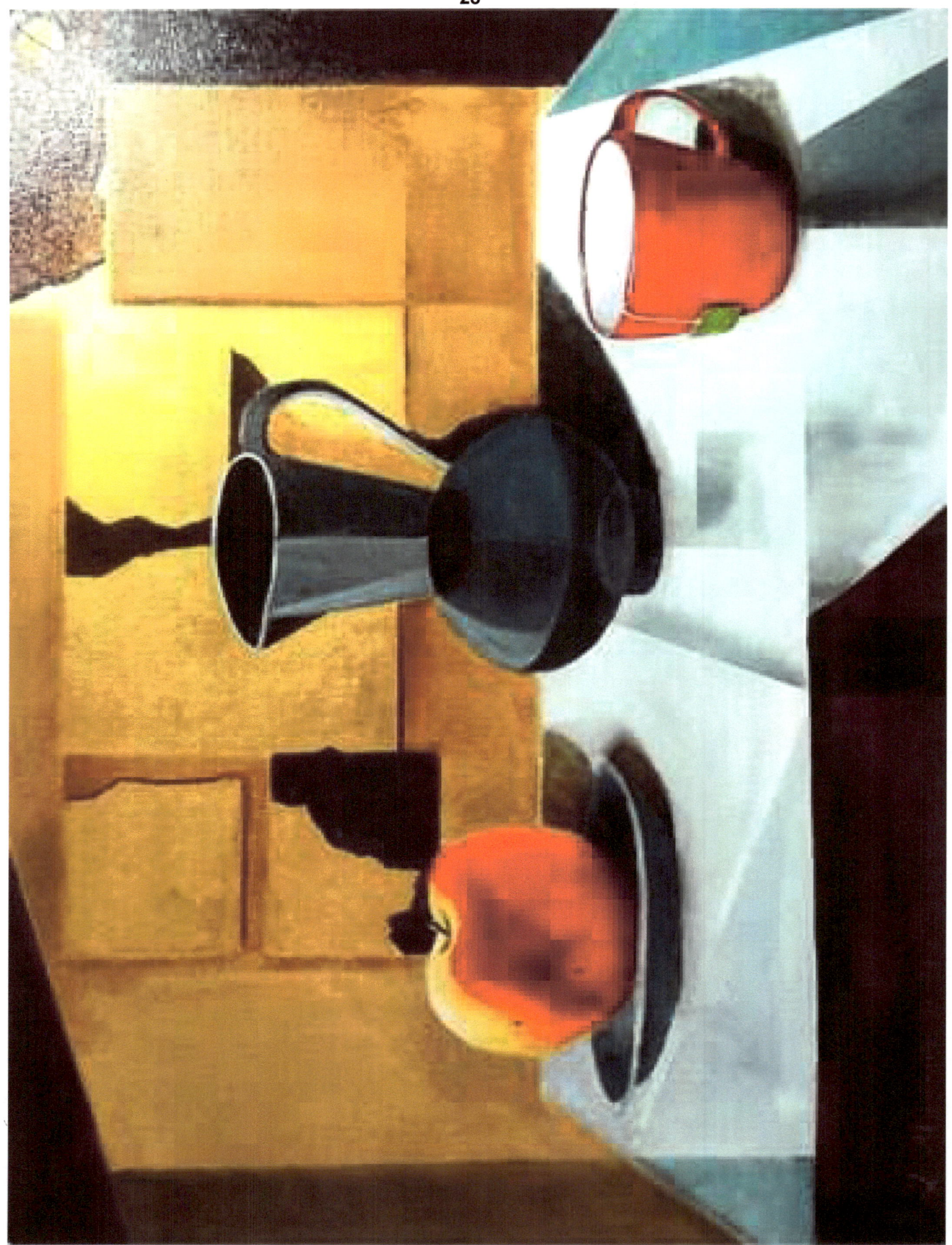

A Khristina Reed Manansala Painting

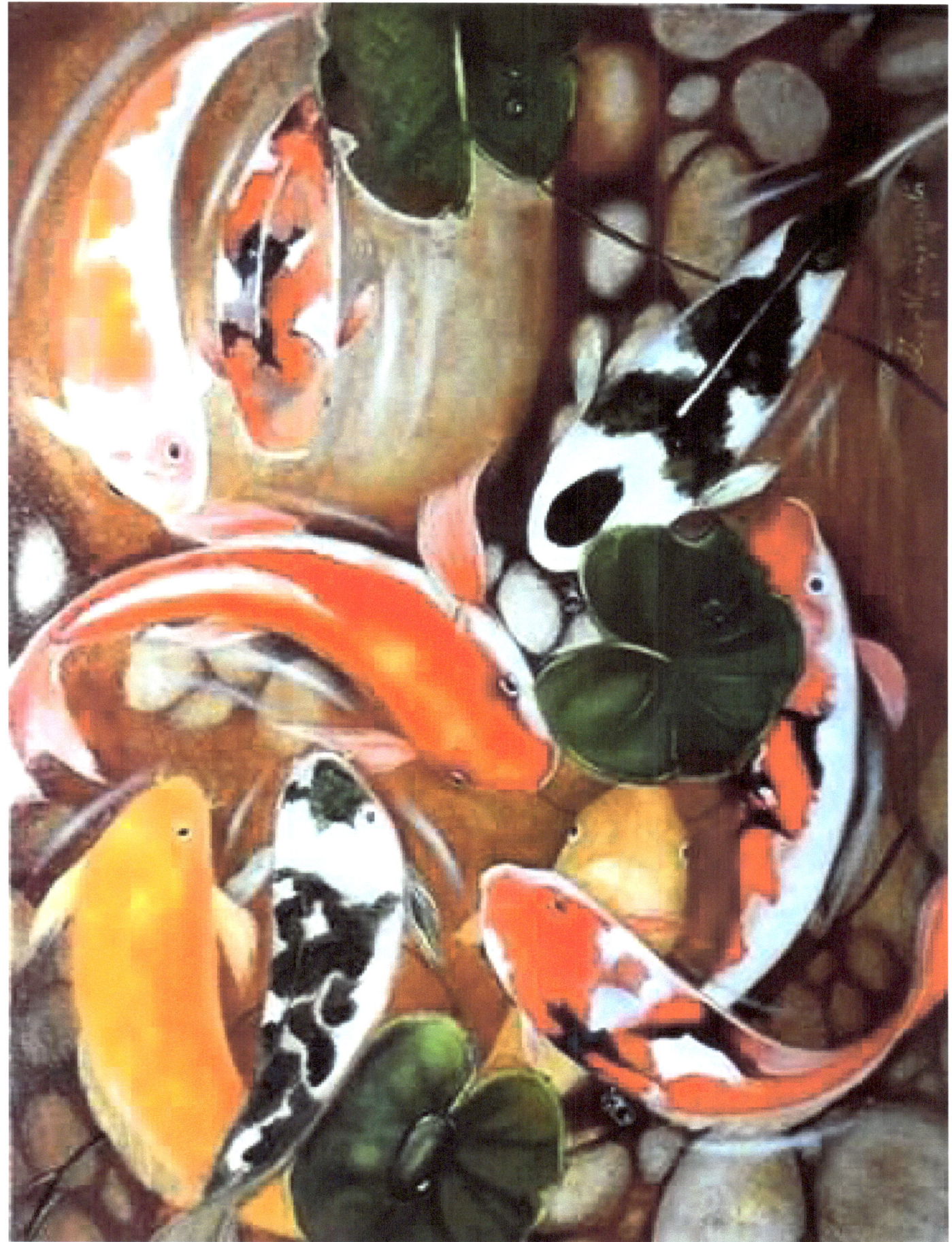

A Khristina Reed Manansala Painting

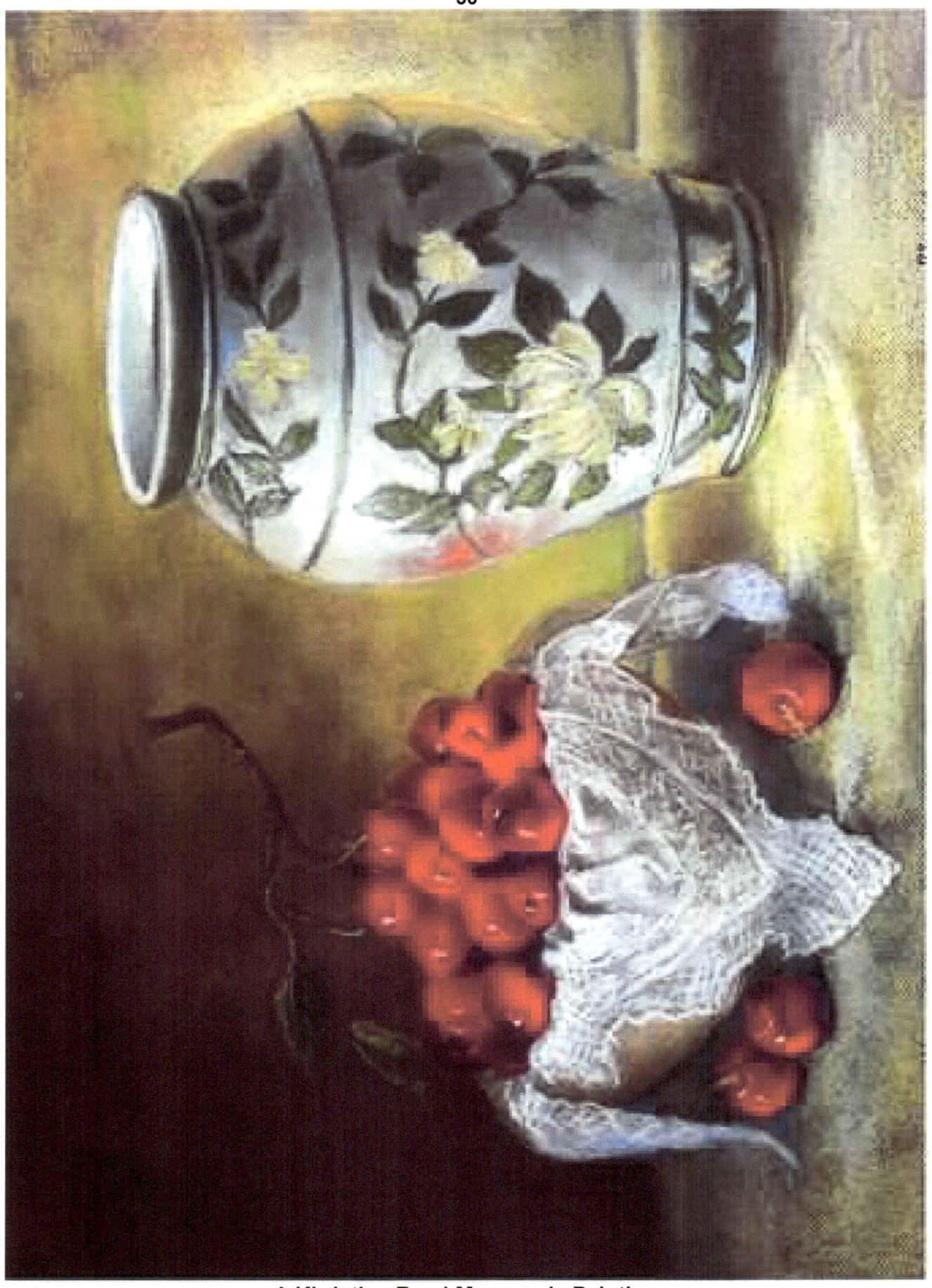

A Khristina Reed Manansala Painting

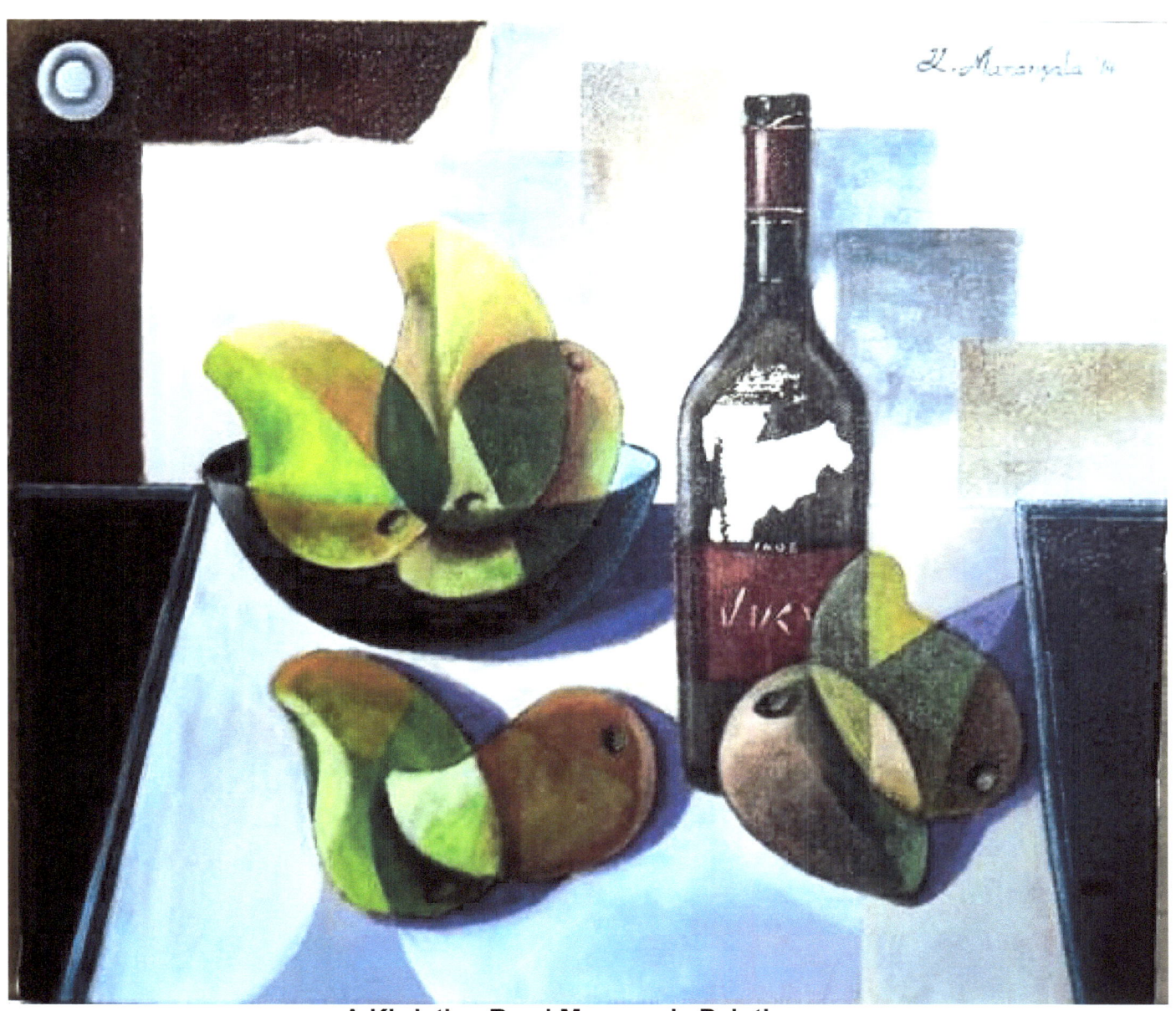

A Khristina Reed Manansala Painting

Thank You and Welcome! Khristina Reed Manansala is a grand-daughter of the Philippine National Artist Vicente Manansala, the famous mural painter and abstract illustrator. This art book is suitable as coffee table book to entertain friends. Viewers can order the actual paintings from Khristina in Manila. She is also ready to do commission works. Each page is 8.5x11 inches, and can be cut out for framing.

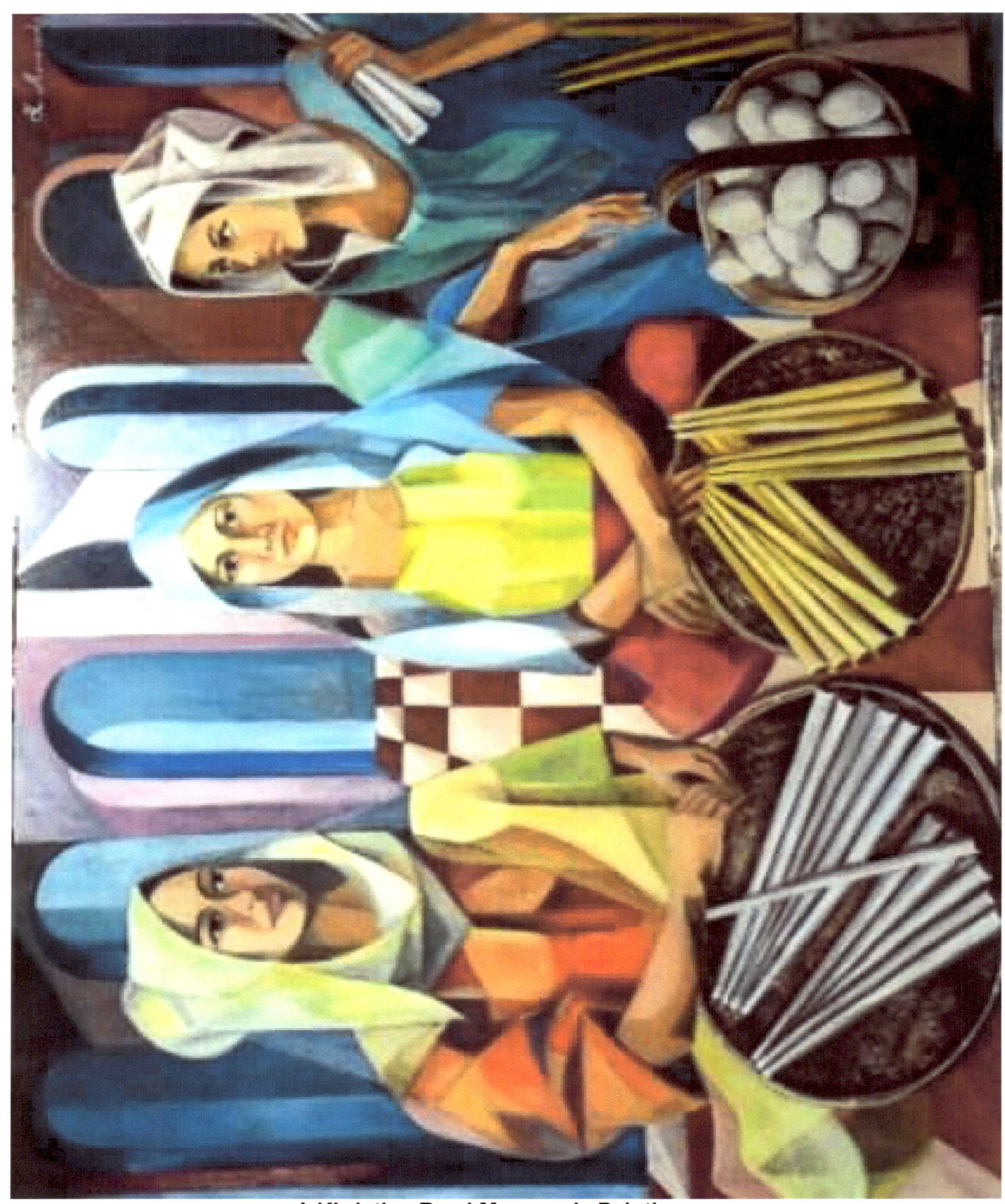

A Khristina Reed Manansala Painting

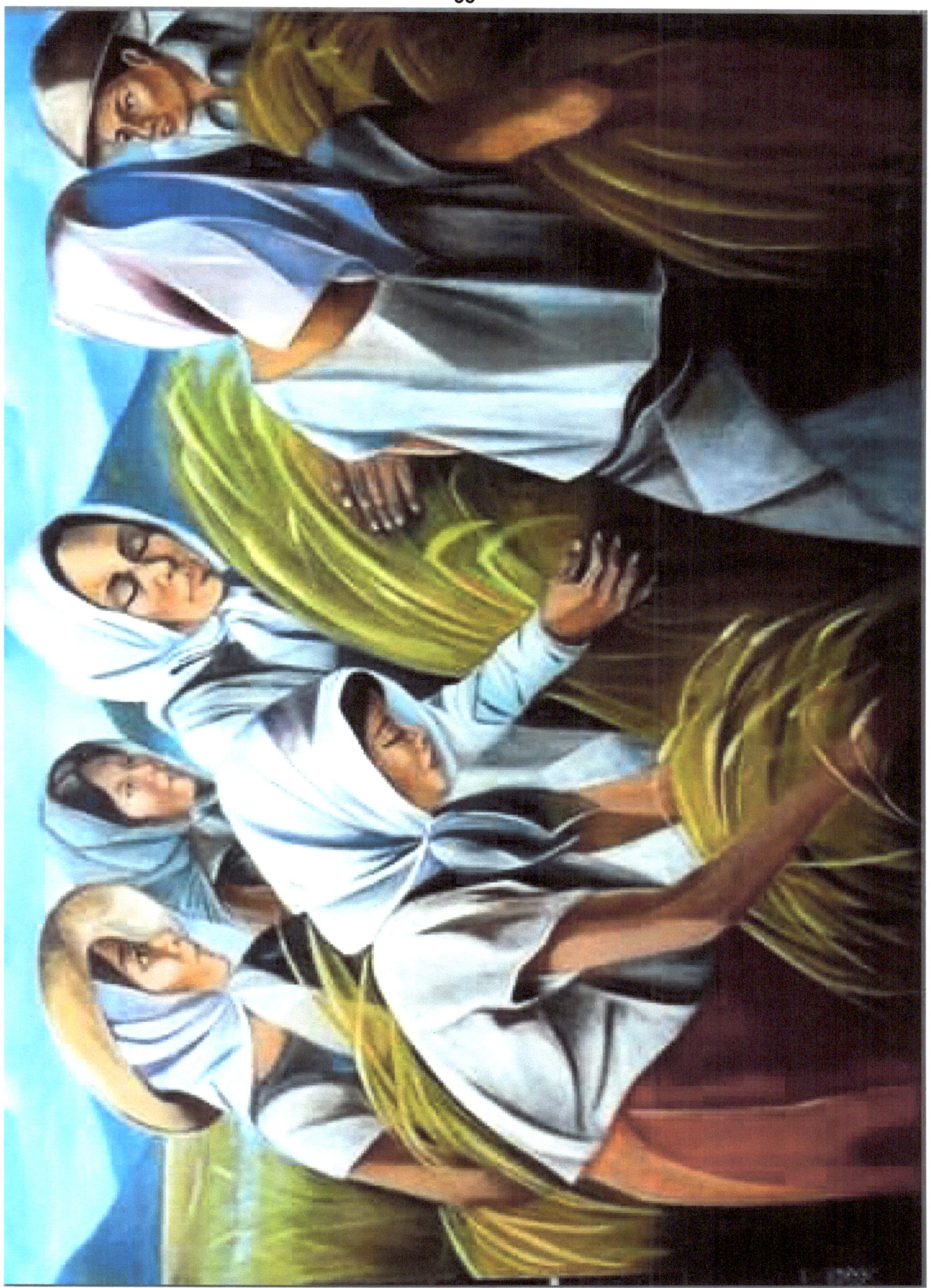

A Khristina Reed Manansala Painting

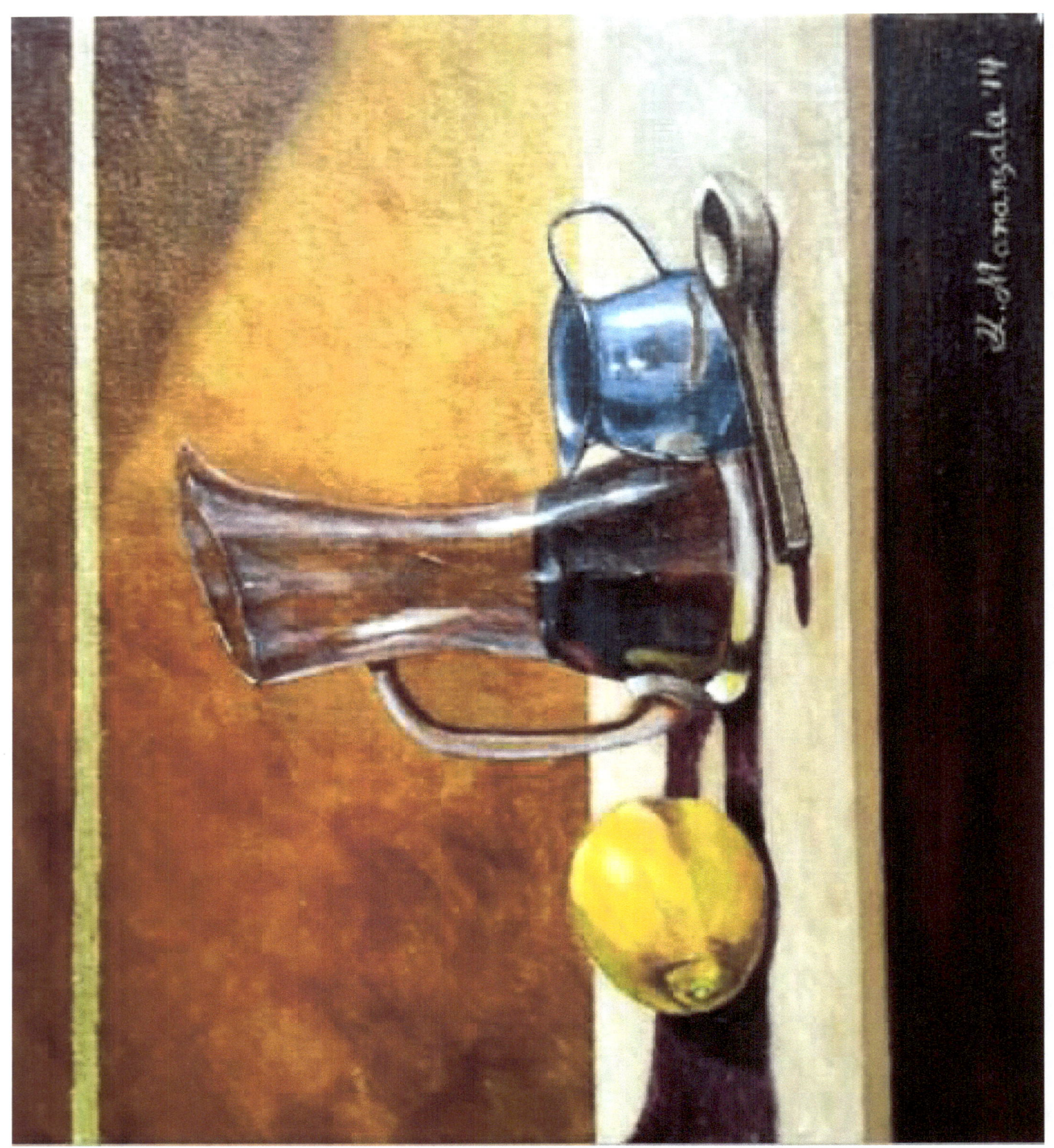

A Khristina Reed Manansala Painting

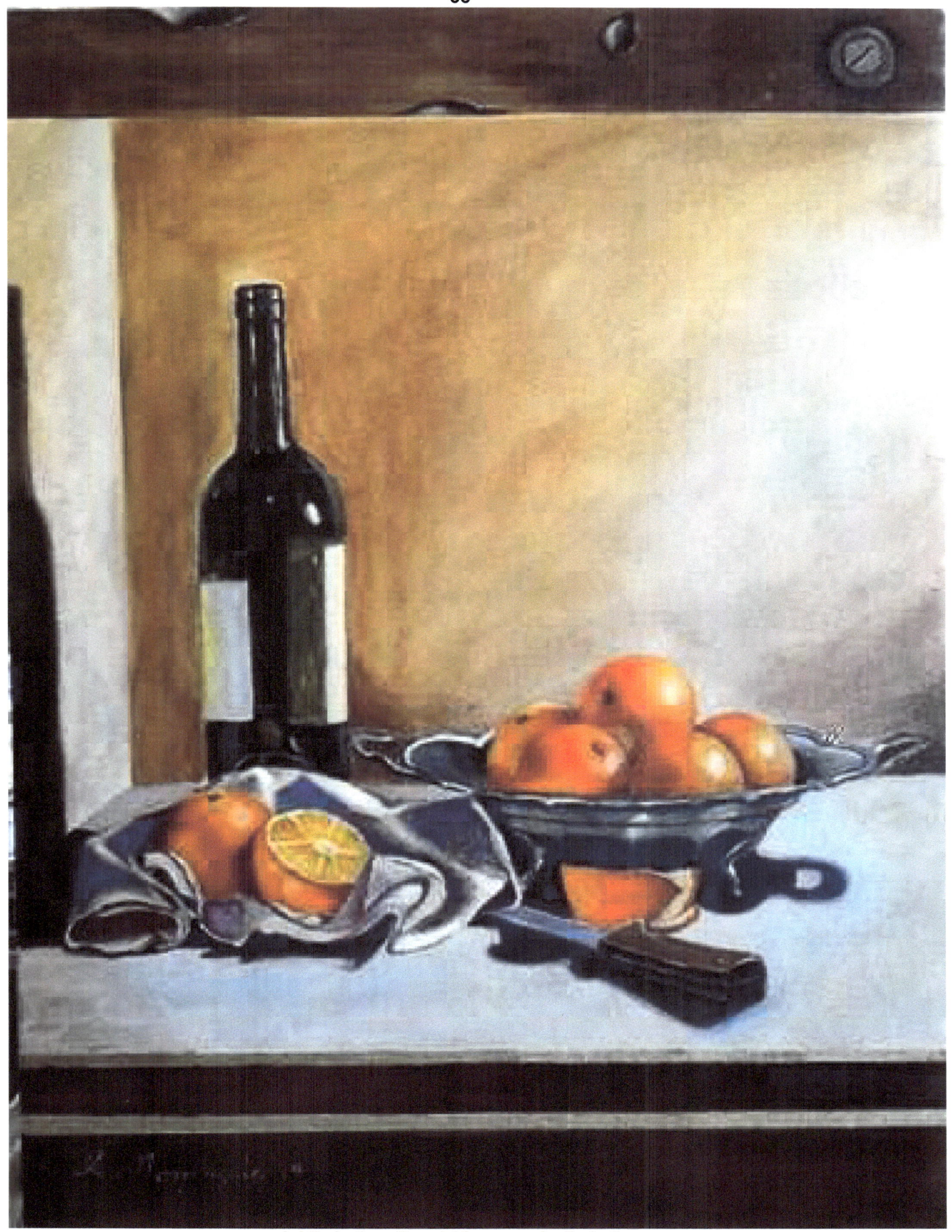

A Khristina Reed Manansala Painting

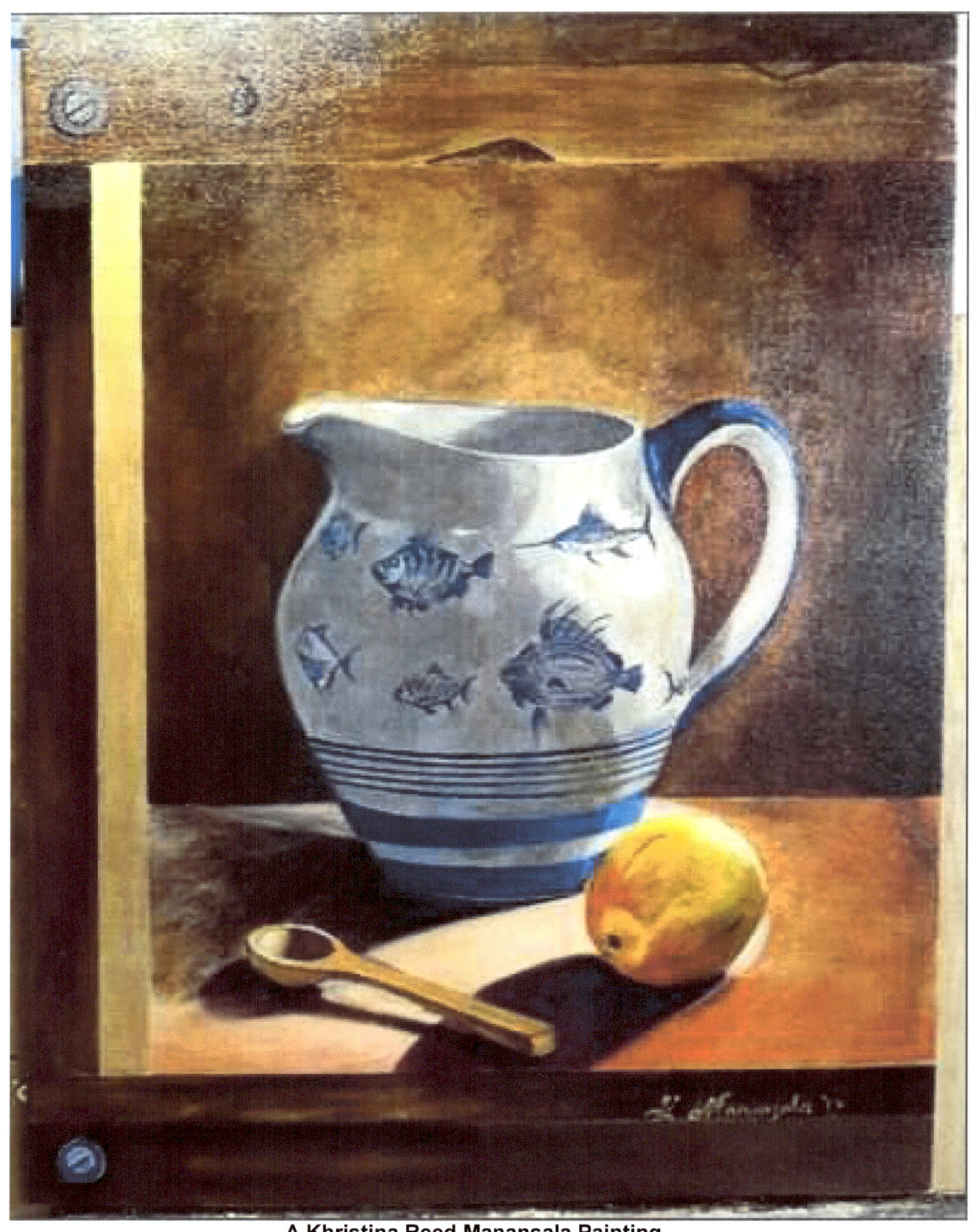

A Khristina Reed Manansala Painting

37

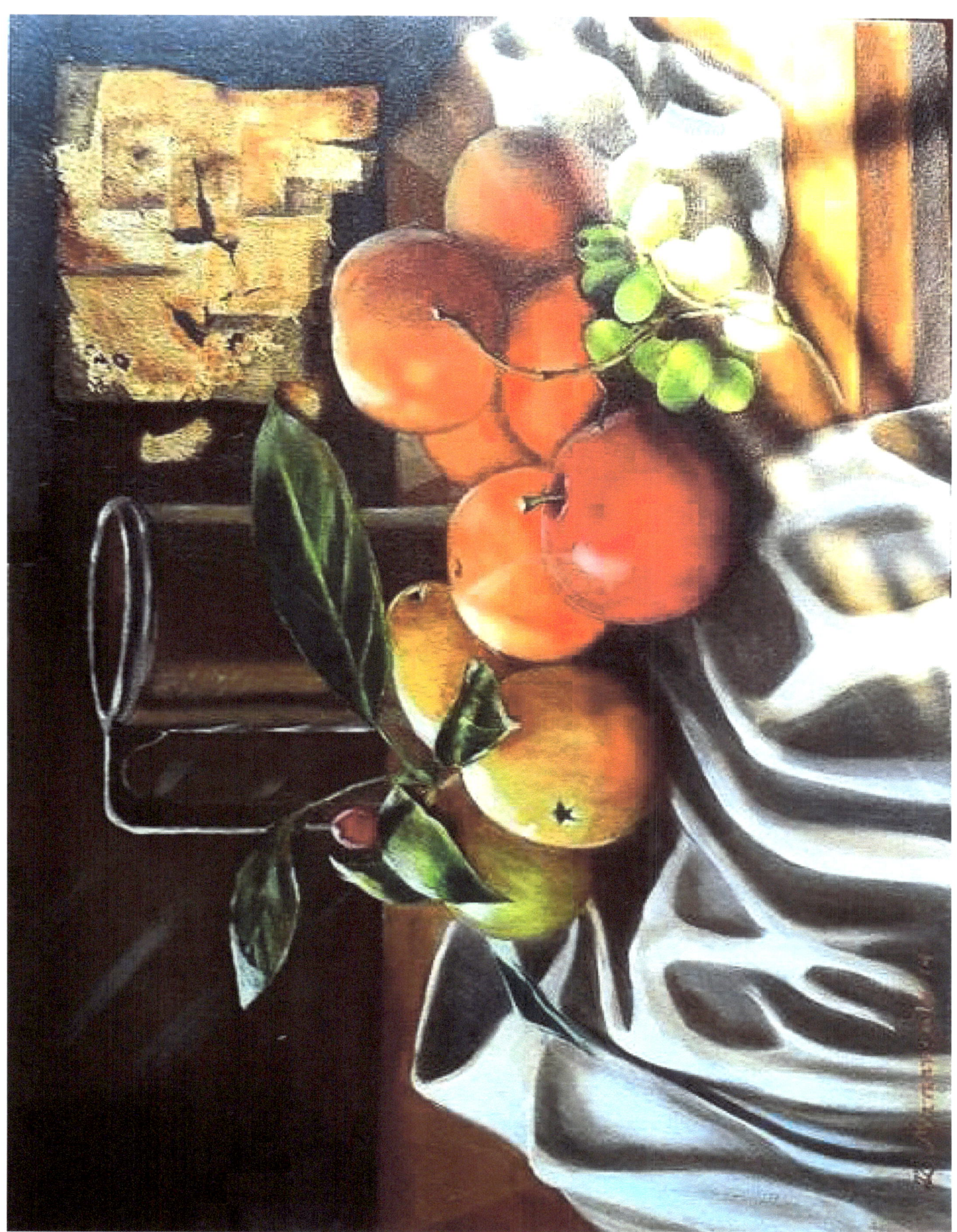

A Khristina Reed Manansala Painting

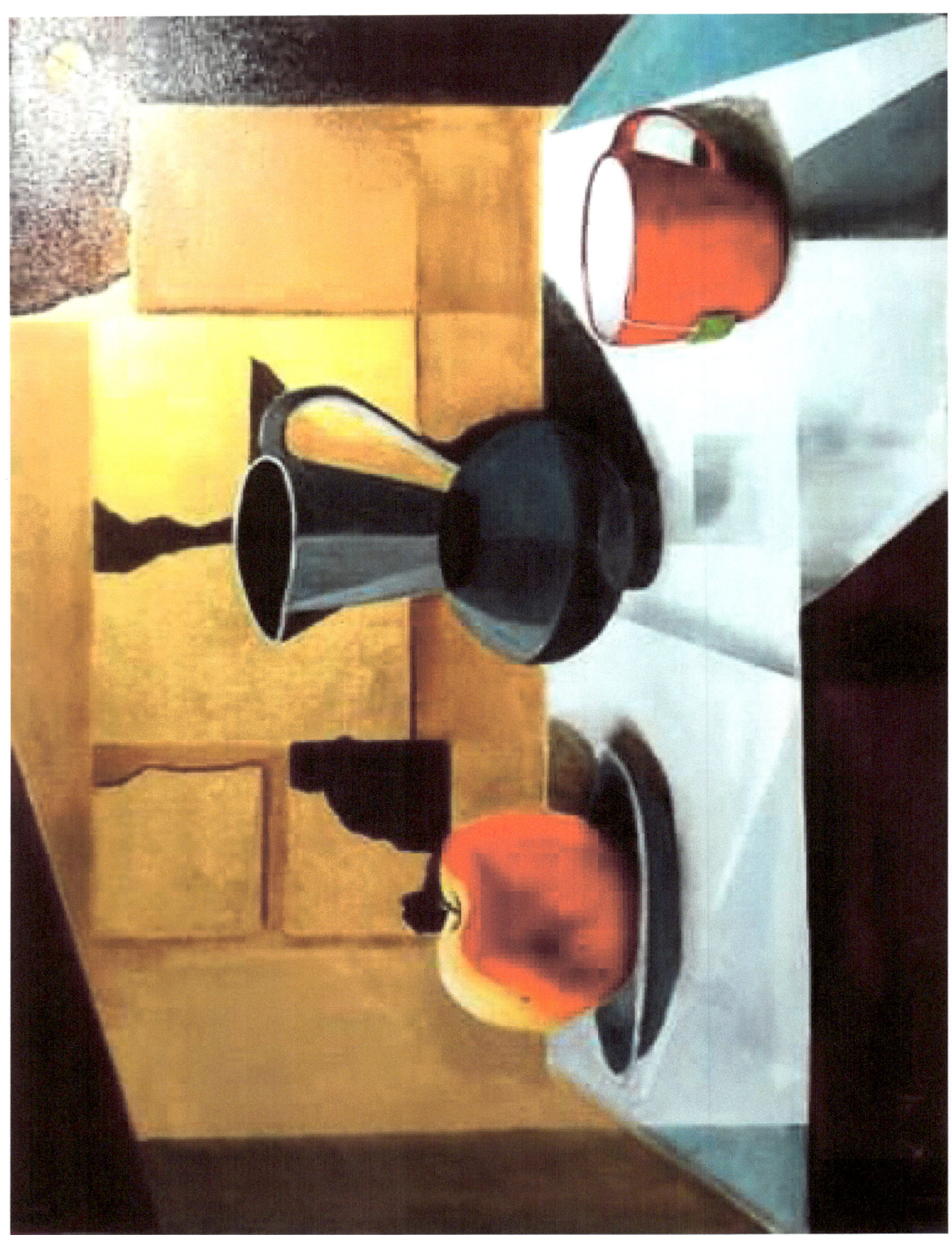

A Khristina Reed Manansala Painting

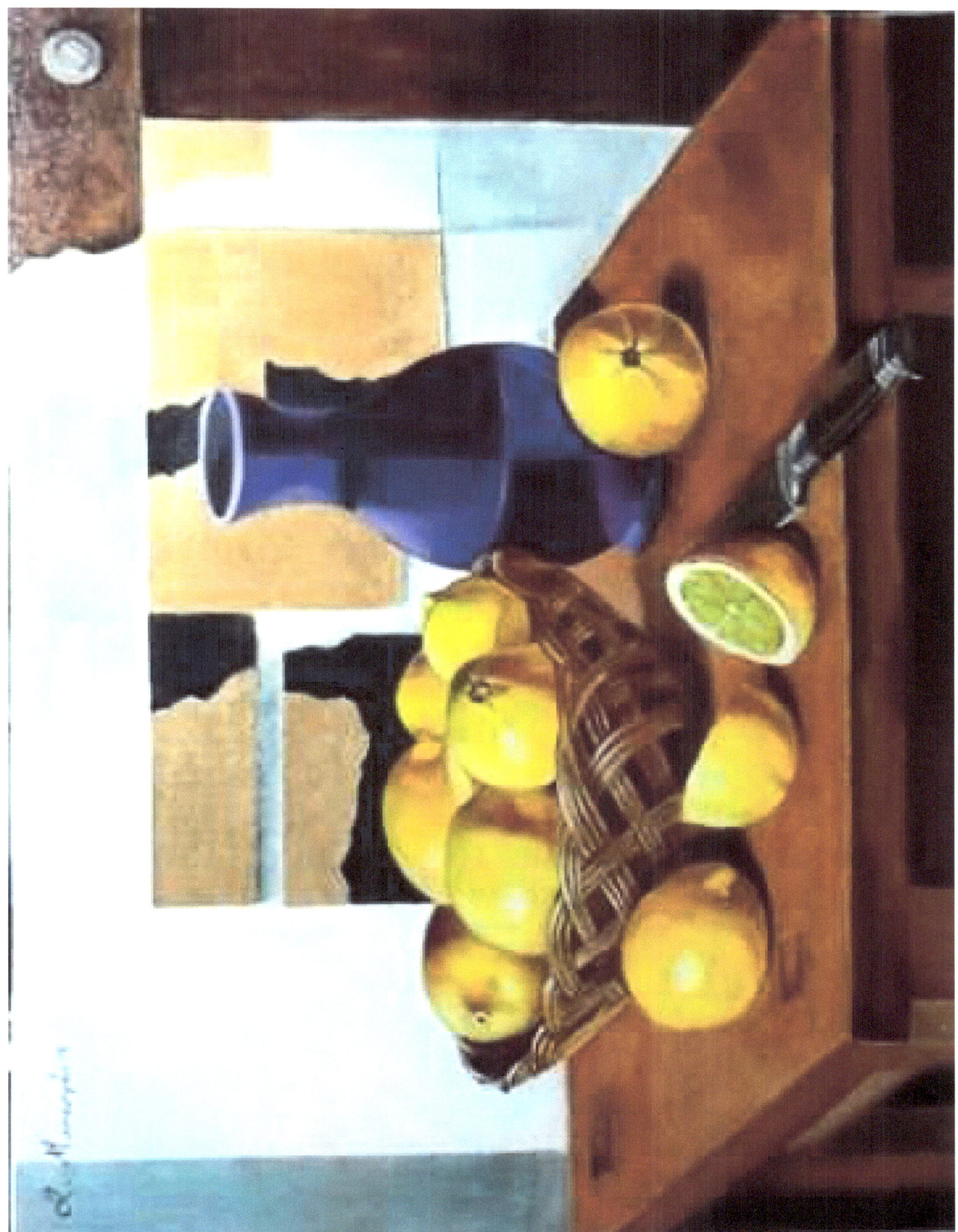

A Khristina Reed Manansala Painting

Publisher's List - Buy online as paperback or kindle, contact
job_elizes@yahoo.com, tatay@usa.com

Writings 1 Book, 2012 , Articles by Bambi Harper + Butch Jiimenez + Dr. Phil Stack + Noel Alegre + Toto Causing +_ Melanie Ferrer + Susie Barbieri _ Rodel Ramos + Sylvia Salvador + Tatay Jobo Elizes + + **Writings 2 Book, 2012,** Artices by Gov. Grace Padaca + Melanie Aquino + Toto Causing + Rodel Rodis + Cesar Torres + Joey Concepcion + Charity Guides + Cesar Lumba +_ Casiano Mayor Jr. + Sonny Coloma + Anonymous.+ + **Writings 3A Book, 2012**, Articles by Norman Madrid + Dr. Rene Azurin + Ernie Delfin + Toto Causing + Dr. Jose Abueva + MarVic Cagurangan + Casiano Mayor Jr + Rod Garcia + Roy Gaane + Tatay Jobo Elizes + + **Writings 3B Book, 2012**, Articles by Ceres Busa + John Reyes + Bert Guiang. + + **Writings 4A Book, 2012**, Articles by Dr Jose Abueva + Col. Dennis Acop + Fred Natividad + Irineo P. Goce + KaPule2 + Miguel Reynadlo + Marjorie Ann Elizes Reyes+ + **Writings 4B Book, 2012**, 1. Mi Ultimo Adios (My Last Farewell), *Dr. Jose P. Rizal* + 2. Aling Pagibig Sa Tinubuang Bayan, *Gat. Andres Bonifacio* + Articles by Irineo P. Goce or KaPule2 + + **Writings 5 Book - "Best Hopes" 2010 (About President P-Noy)**, Articles by Tony Meloto + F.SionilJose + Juan L. Mercado + OFWs Letter + Marcelo Tecson + Cesar Torres+ Perry Diaz + Dr. Philip S. Chua + Ernie Delfin + Atty. Ted Laguatan + Frank Wenceslao Jaileen F. Jimeno + Tatay Jobo Elizes + + **Writings 6 Book, 2010** + I. SONA - State Of Nation Address - English - *Pres. Benigno Aquino III* + II. SONA - State of Nation Address - Pilipino - *Pres. Benigno Aquino III* + III. First 100 Days peech - Pilipino - *Pres. Benigno Aquino III* + *Artiucles by Bert Guiang + Tony Meloto + Felicito or Tong C. Payumo + Cesar Lumba + Flor Lacanilao + Juan DelaCruz or Txtmanika + Dr. Ramon Marquez + Joey Jamito + Percival Cruz + Rod Garcia + Orion Perez Dumdum + Sarah Raymundo.* + + **Writings 7 Book, 2010** - My Vintage Pics - Pictorials & Family, Tatay Jobo Elizes + + **Writings 8 Book, 2010**, Articles by Gel Santos Relos + Ms.Mike Portes + Jose Ma. Montelibano + Tony Meloto + Dr. Philip S. Chua + Dr. Cesar D. Candari + Dr. Eliseo Serina + Greg B. Macabenta + Irineo P. Goce or KaPule2 + Percival Cruz + Juan DelaCruz or Textmani + Demosthenes B. Donato. + + **Writings 9 Book, April 2011**, Articles by Judge Simeon dumdum Jr + Gemma Cruz Araneta + Larry Henares Jr + Tony Joaquin + Allen Gaborro + Atty. Toto Causing + Mar-Vic Cagurangn + Emily Espanol Derry, Poet + Elyn Jean Felarca, Poet + Naysan A. Albaytar + Laura Wade, Blogger + Perter Allan Mariano + Marge Trajeco-Aberasturi + Julia Carreon Lagoc + Irineo P. Goce or KaPulle2 + Anonymous. + + **Writings 10 Book, July, 2010**, Articles by Atty.Ted Lagutan + Percival C. Cruz + Allen Gaborro + Peter Allan Mariano + M.L. Munoz + Alvib T. Tabaniag + Resty Odon + Dr. Phili S. Chua + Dr. Cesar D. Candari + Anonymous. + + **Writings 11 Book, August, 2011** + 1, SONA In English and Filipino, by President Benigno Aquino III (P-Noy) + 2, Telltale Signs: SONA and the Dogfight Over Spratlys, by Rodel Rodis + Atty. Ted Laguatan + Tatay Jobo Elizes + Jeremiah M. Opiniano + OFW Journalists + Bob & Carol Hammerslag + Roger P. Olivares + Rob Ceralvo + Anonymous + Irineo P. Goce or KaPule2 + Random. + + **Writings 12 Book, April 2012** + Articles By Orion Perez Dumdum + Julia C. Lagoc + Honorio M. Cruz, MD + Ben Gonzales, MD + Mar-Vic Cagurangan + Marisa Lerias + Gerry Partido + Dr. Cesar D. Candari + Erwin De Leon + Jovelyn B. Revilla + Tatay Jobo Elizes + + **Writings 13 Book, July 2012** + Articles by Raymundo E. Narag + M.L. Munoz + Sonia Barbara gl Munoz + Pamela Joy Agtoto + Percival C. Cruz + Tatay Jobo Elizes + Jhakie Eslit Bayobay + Reygel Saplad Perales.

Timely Writings 14, 2013 + Articles by Cesar F. Lumba + Eugenio Pulmano + Late Jesse Robredo + Antonio Nievera + Alvin T. Tabaniag + Kevin L. Nadal + Anonymous + Fred Natividad + Anonymous + Ellen Tordesillas + Lat Capt. Rene N. Jarque + + **Timeless Writings-15 (TW15), 2014** + Articles by SC Justice Antonio T. Carpio + Atty Dodel Rodis + Atty. Ted Laguatan + Sona by Pres. Benigno Aquino III + F. Sionil Jose + Dr. Philipi Stack + Racz Kelly, Padilla + Bert Armada.

Solo Authored Books: + + +

Book A, **Turning Points**, *Job Elizes Sr,1968 (Reissue 2009)* + + + Book B, **Be Considerate For Once**, *Tatay Jobo Elizes (Jr), 2013* Book C, **Piglets Unlimited - Wealth**, *Tatay Jobo Elizes, 2009* + + + Book D, **Out of the Misty Sea We Must**, *Cesar Lumba, 2010* + + + Book E, **Fulfilled** – *Gonzales Reynaldo, Editor, 2010* + + + Book F - **Reflections** - *Bert Guiang, 2010* + + + Book G, **Writings 7 - My Vintage Pics**, *Tatay Jobo Elizes, 2010* + Book H, **May Bagwis Ang Pag-ibig**, *Percival C. Cruz* + + + Book I, **Letters To Matrimony**, *Irineo P. Goce, Ka Pule2, 2011* + Book J, **Songs I Wish You Knew**, *Soledad R. Juan, 2011* + + + Book K, **Make My Day**, *Larry Henares Jr., 1993, Re-issue 2011* + Book L, **Our Guerrero Family**, *Tatay Jobo Elizes, 2010* + + + Book M, **Handy Jokes**, *Tatay J. Elizes, 2011* + Book N, **FaveArt 1**, *Tatay Jobo Elizes, 2011* + + Book O, **Beyond idle thoughts**, *MLMunoz, Sept,2011* + + + Book P, **Cracks In The Armor**, *Mariano Ngan, Oct 2011* + + + Book Q, **FaveArt 2**, *Tatay Jobo Elizes, 2011* + + Book R, **Balitang Kutsero**, *Perry Diaz, Jan 2012* + + + Book S, **FaveArt3**, *Tatay Jobo, 2011* + + + Book T, **FaveArt4** ,*2012, Tatay Jobo* + + Book U, **Stack Family Journals**, *Phil & Fe Stack, 2012* + + + Book V, **Emily, An Adoption Journey**, *Romerl Elizes, 2012* + + + Book W, **Hermes Alegre Art Gallery**, *TJ & Hermes, 2012* + + + Book X, **Masaya Din, Malungkot Din**, *Jovelyn B. Revilla, 2012* Book Y, **Tiis, Sipag At Tiyaga**, *Raquel Delfin Padilla, 2012* + + + Book Z, **Until I Meet You**, *Jhackie Eslit Bayobay, 2012* + + + Book AA, **Buhay At Pag-ibig**, *Argel Lucero Tamayo, 2012* + + + Book AB, **Hail to the Second Best**, *Dr. Philip Stack, 2012* + + + Book AC, **Life Bus**, *Mommy Joyce Pineda-Faulmino, 2012* + + + Book AD, **My Candid Musings**, *Monette Dioquino Calugay, 2012* + + + Book AE, **Tickets to Life**, *Maria Lourdes Jesalva, 2012* + + + Book AF, **The Dove Files**, *Mike Portes, 2012* + + + Book AG, **Nursing Vignettes**, *Jocelyn Cerrudo Sese, 2012* + Book AH, **Poor Ba Us**, *R.A. Gubalane, 2012* + + + Book AI, **Summer Idyll**, *Avelina Gil, 2012* + + Book AJ, **Legacy (Pamana)**, *Rachel Astrero, 2012* + + Book AK, **Narratives Old & New**, *Avelina J. Gil, 2013* + + Book AL, **Buhay Saudi**, *Adele J. Esic, 2013* + + Book AM, **Buhay Ofw Atbp**, *Jessica Napat, 2013* + + Book AN, **Mga Tula Ng Buhay**, *Angelita C. Esguerra, 2013* + + Book AO, **Not by Bread Alone**, *Judge Lily V. Magtolis, 2013* + Book AP, **Jokes Collection-2**, *Tatay Jobo Elizes, 2013* + + + Book AR, **My Writings Sometimes**, *Tatay Jobo Elizes, 2013* + Book AS, **Sa 'Yo Na Ako**, *Shayne A. Martinez, 2013* + + Book AT, **My Kin's Family Trees**, *Tatay Jobo Elizes, 2013* + Book AU, **Rizal Family Tree & Others**, *Tatay Jobo Elizes, 2013* + Book AV, **Make My Day-2, Nice & Nasty**, *L. Henares, 2013 (1993)* + Book AW, **Make My Day-3, Cecilia, Love**, *L.Henares, 2013 (1993)*Book AX, **Handy Lyrics-1**, *Tatay Jobo Elizes, 2013* + + Book AY, **Ang Biblos**, *Rev. Dr. Eugenio Guerrero, 2014 (1929)* + + Book AZ, **Make My Day-4, Sweet & Sour**, *L. Henares, 2014 (1993)* + + Book BA, **Life's Journey, True Stories**, *Dr. Phil Stack, 2014* + + Book BB, **Gerry Gil Writings, 2014**, *Danny Gil* + + Book BC, **Mr. President**, *Hermie Rotea, 2014* + + Book BD, **Nostalgic Pics 1**, *Tatay Jobo Elizes, 2014* + + Book BE, **MakeMyDay-5, Saints & Sinners**, *Henares, 2014 (1993)* + + Book BF, **MakeMyDay-6, Villains & Heroes**, *Henares, 2014 (1993)* + + Book BG, **Nostalgic Pics 2 (ElizesClan)**, *TatayJE, 2014* + + Book BH, **MakeMyDay-7, Tough & Tender**, *Henares, 2014(1993)* + + Book BI, **MakeMyDay-8, Light & Shadow**, *Henares, 2014(1993)* + + Book BJ, **MakeMyDay-9, Give & Take**, *Henares, 2014(1993)* + + Book BK, **MakeMyDay-10, ToBeOrNotToBe**, *Henares, 2014(1993)* + Book BL,**Emily Forever In Love, Poems**,*Emily Espanol Derry, 2013* + + Book BM, **The Sinatra Songbook**, *Henares, 2014* + + Book BN, **The Gaborro Reader**, *Allen Gaborro, 2010* + + *Book BO*, Ramon H. Lopez - **Art Gallery**, *2014* + + Book BP, **Philippines Via Old Pics-1**, *Tatay Jobo, 2014* + + Book BQ, **Ronna Manansala - Art Gallery**, *2014* + + Book BR, **Philippines Via Old Pics-2**, *Tatay Jobo, 2014* + + Book BS, **Being Good-A Medley Of Love**, *Dr. Phil Stack, 2014* + + Book BT, **Lifestream Fisherman, A Filipino Odyssey**, *Paul Dalde, Jul2014* + + Book BU, **Kristina Reed Manansala, Art Gallery-1**, *August 2014.*

Publisher: Tatay Jobo Elizes was born in Manila, Philippines, in 1934, retiree, now based in NY, busy self-publishing and involved in piglets dispersal programs.
Acknowledgement & Dedication: Gratitude and acknowledgment belongs to those who support my hobby publishing books and charities. I heartily dedicate this to my wife, **Cora**, my children, **Tetchie, Chevy & Abeth, and Marie & Bimbo**, my grandchildren, **Karines & Aung, Noelle, Chad, Marjo, Jeb, Marvin & Marty**, great-grandson **Jason Win** and **Carson**, my siblings **Susan, Hilda, Bobby, Bey & Manny** and to all my extended relatives and to all Filipinos.
ISBN Code. Printed in the United States of America under ISBN code below.
ISBN-13: 978 - 1501007262   + + +   ISBN-10: 1501007262

Publisher's List - Contact job_elizes@yahoo.com, tatay@usa.com
My websites: http://tinyurl.com/mj76ccq + + + www.jobelizes.com
"Buy A Book or Gift Somebody - paperback or kindle edition online"